Gyo Obata／HOK

ギョー・オバタ 1954–1990

Gyo Obata／HOK

ギョー・オバタ 1954–1990

Architecture and Urbanism

1990 December Extra Edition
Gyo Obata／HOK

1990年12月臨時増刊号
ギョー・オバタ 1954—1990

Publisher: Yoshio Yoshida
Editor: Toshio Nakamura
Design Consultant: Massimo Vignelli
Printed in Japan
Published by a+u Publishing Co.,Ltd.
30-8, Yushima 2-chome, Bunkyo-ku, Tokyo, 113, Japan
Phone: (03) 816-2935, FAX: (03) 816-2937
Distributor: The Japan Architect Co.,Ltd.
31-2, Yushima 2-chome, Bunkyo-ku, Tokyo, 113, Japan
Price Outside Japan: ¥5,800＋¥1,500 (seamail postage)

4
Editor's Introduction
6
Statement
Gyo Obata
10
Essay: Not Stylistic But Attitudinal
George McCue
16
A Look at HOK
20
Introduction to Projects

Works:
22
Priory Chapel
28
Carrier Chapel, Mississippi University for Women
32
National Air and Space Museum
40
King Saud University
48
George R. Moscone Convention Center
58
Dallas Galleria
66
King Khalid International Airport
72
St. Louis Union Station
78
BP America, Inc., Corporate Headquarters
84
Kellogg Company Corporate Headquarters

© a+u 建築と都市
発行日：1990年12月20日
発行者：吉田義男
編集者：中村敏男
デザイン・コンサルタント：マッシモ・ヴィネリ
定価4800円 (本体4660円)／送料360円
振替：東京3-98119
発行所：株式会社エー・アンド・ユー
〒113 東京都文京区湯島2-30-8
電話：(03)816-2935 (代)，FAX：(03)816-2937
印刷所：大日本印刷株式会社
大取次：東販・日販・大阪屋・中央社・栗田出版・誠光堂
禁無断転載

4
編集者序
6
ステイトメント
ギョー・オバタ
10
評論：ギョー・オバタの目指す建築
ジョージ・マッキュー
16
設計組織 HOK の有機的な構造
20
HOK のプロジェクト

作品：
22
プライアリー・チャペル
28
ミシシッピ女子大学キャリア・チャペル
32
国立航空宇宙博物館
40
キング・サウド大学
48
ジョージ・R・モスコーン・コンヴェンション・センター
58
ダラス・ガレリア
66
キング・ハリド国際空港
72
セントルイス・ユニオン駅
78
BP アメリカ社本社ビル
84
ケロッグ社本社ビル

92
Fairmont Hotel, San Jose
98
Fairmont Hotel, Chicago
104
Burger King Corporation World Headquarters
114
World Bank "J" Building
120
Joe Robbie Stadium
126
Bradley Center Arena
132
Pilot Field
138
Kansai International Airport Design Competition
142
Metropolitan Square
152
The Living World／St. Louis Zoo
162
AmSouth／Harbert Plaza Mixed Use Center
168
801 Grand Avenue
172
Academic Research Building,
J. Hillis Miller Health Center
178
Columbia University Center for Engineering and
Physical Science Research
182
Wells Fargo Center at Capitol Mall
186
Minami Office Tower

190
Camden Yards Twin-Stadium Complex
192
Cervantes Convention Center Expansion and Domed Stadium
196
The Temple:
Reorganized Church of Jesus Christ of Latter Day Saints
200
Kings County Hospital Center
204
Brickell Gateway
208
Retirement Park at Tokushima Prefecture
210
New York Hospital
214
Northwest Airlines World Travel Center
218
Foley Square

224
Biography of Gyo Obata
226
Chronological List of Gyo Obata／HOK: 1954-
236
Members of HOK

Front cover: Gyo Obata
Back cover: 801 Grand Avenue
Photo by Robert Pettus

92
サンノゼ・フェアモント・ホテル
98
シカゴ・フェアモント・ホテル
104
バーガー・キング社世界本社
114
世界銀行「J」ビルディング
120
ジョー・ロビー・スタジアム
126
ブラッドレー・センター・アリーナ
132
パイロット・フィールド
138
関西国際空港旅客ターミナル・ビル設計競技案
142
メトロポリタン・スクエア・オフィス・タワー
152
セントルイス動物園リヴィング・ワールド
162
アムサウス／ハーバード・プラザ多目的センター
168
801グランド・アヴェニュー・オフィス・タワー
172
J・ヒリス・ミラー医療センター学術研究所
178
コロンビア大学工学自然科学研究センター
182
キャピトル・モール・ウェルズ・ファーゴ・センター
186
ミナミ・オフィス・タワー
190
カムデン・ヤーズ・ツイン・スタジアム

192
セルヴァンテス・コンヴェンション・センター増築およびドーム・スタジアム
196
ザ・テンプル：末日聖徒イエス・キリスト改革教会世界本部
200
キングス・カウンティ・ホスピタル・センター
204
ブリッケル・ゲートウェイ
208
徳島県高齢者村マスター・プラン
210
ニューヨーク・ホスピタル
214
ノースウェスト航空ワールド・トラヴェル・センター
218
フォーリィ・スクエア

224
ギョー・オバタ略歴
226
ギョー・オバタ／HOK作品年譜：1954-
236
HOKスタッフ・リスト

表紙：ギョー・オバタ
裏表紙：801グランド・アヴェニュー・オフィス・タワー

Editor's Introduction

編集者序

Hellmuth Obata & Kassabaum (HOK) has the second highest annual earnings among architectural design firms of the world, offices in San Francisco, Los Angeles, Washington D.C., New York, London, Saudi Arabia, Hong Kong, the list goes on, and a total of 1084 employees. The head office remains in St. Louis, Missouri, the city founded in the eighteenth century by Frenchmen as the base for their fur trade. St. Louis has grown beside the Mississippi into a great modern city with Eero Saarinen's Thomas Jefferson Memorial Arch the fitting symbol of its dignity. HOK has designed many office buildings and much public architecture in the city making significant contributions to its growth. It was HOK that designed improvements and restoration for the stone architecture of the Union Station in the center of the city, which with the waning of the railroad had fallen into dilapidation, adding a shopping mall and a hotel and reviving its popularity.

The name HOK may suggest Houston's The Galleria to some people. Some may think of the National Air and Space Museum in Washington D.C.; others of the Dallas/Fort Worth International Airport. Some of them will also be reminded of the King Khalid International Airport in Riyadh, Saudi Arabia. HOK's design achievements do not just extend geographically at home and abroad. Company head office, general office, and commercial buildings; educational, health and medical, and public and transportation facilities: their range covers so many of the fields of architecture and types of structure.

At the top of the firm stands Gyo Obata. Participating in all projects and involved in all departments of the corporate structure, he is the firm's organizational and architectural leader. In contrast to the other large architectural firms in America, departments are not lead by different specialists in the respective building fields. Obata controls all projects. Organization theory suggests that organizations are social structures created by individuals for the purpose of collaborative pursuit of specified common goals.

Obata seeks to encompass this kind of social and collaborative system within his own capacity as an architect. He is not influenced by fashionable styles or current trends. Viewed from the stand point of architectural style, the works of HOK do not depart from modernism. Whether structures in wood, clad in bricks or tiles, or covered with glass or metal skins, their forms are not dressed up in styles. HOK uses contemporary materials in contemporary engineering techniques to design the most appropriate structure for the given program. Obata does not set out to express his individuality as an architect in form and style, but rather to find expression in the process and stages from design to realization. Sometimes HOK's architecture is criticized as not having any style at all. Those who make such comments would find in it the rigorous application of integrating design principles not restricted to any given style or formalism if they would take the time to observe HOK's works carefully.

Gyo Obata describes himself as a "people-oriented architect." He says buildings must be created according to people's patterns of movement and behavior. One can easily see how this works in The Galleria, for instance. Or in the Dallas/Fort Worth International Airport. Or in the National Air and Space Museum in Washington D.C. None of these would have succeeded without minute and detailed research on users' movements and activities within such facilities. Not just horizontal movements either; they pay just as much attention to the vertical circulation patterns. That's why their high-rise office buildings work so well. Looking at HOK's architecture, one realizes that this attention to user circulation informs the works in terms of two basic plans: the linear and condensed plans, corresponding to movement, activity and circulation in the horizontal and vertical directions.

One could say that Obata's people-oriented emphasis comes down to a concern for architecture as public form; which is not confined to any simplistic conception of the public significance of architecture. Characteristically such architecture would not be sufficient in its visual impact if it were not endowed with all of the elements of "commoditie, firmness, and delight" required by Henry Wotton in the seventeenth century. Obata understands that architecture constitutes public receptacles. That's why he is not influenced by transitory fads of fashion and popularity; nor does he pander to decoration or excess. What do people want? How do they move? What do they respond to? It is in his answers to these questions that Obata integrates architectural design and all aspects of the organization of Hellmuth Obata & Kassabaum. (Translated by John D. Lamb)

年間世界第二の収益を上げ，サンフランシスコ，ロサンゼルス，ワシントン D.C.，ニューヨーク，さらにロンドン，サウジアラビア，ホンコンなどにも事務所を開いているヘルムース・オバタ・アンド・カサバウム（HOK）の本拠地はミズーリ州セントルイスにある．ミシシッピ川に臨むこの都市の起源は18世紀フランス人による毛皮の交易基地に遡るが，今では河沿いの放物線アーチが象徴するように現代的都市に成長している．HOKもまたこの都市に数多くのオフィス・ビル，公共建築を建て，その発展に貢献している．市の中央にユニオン・ステーションと呼ばれた鉄道駅があったが，鉄道の衰微によって荒廃していたその石造建築の外観や内部を改修して，ショッピング・モールやホテルをつけくわえてふたたび人気を取り戻したのもHOKである．

HOKの名前を聞く時，あるひとはヒューストンのザ・ガレリアを思い起こすかもしれない．また，ワシントン D.C. の国立航空宇宙博物館やダラス・フォート・ワース空港を思い浮かべるかもしれない．なかには，サウジアラビア，リヤドのキング・ハリド空港を挙げるひともいるだろう．このようにHOKの設計は，その場所を国内的，国際的に拡大しているばかりではない．企業の本社ビル，一般のオフィス・ビル，商業ビル，教育施設，保健・医療施設，公共・輸送施設など広範な領域に及んでいる．

現在HOKは1,084名の人員によって会社組織が構成されている．その頂点にいるのがギョー・オバタである．彼はすべてのプロジェクトに関与し，すべてのデパートメントに関係している．彼は会社組織のリーダーであり，設計組織を率いる建築家である．他のアメリカの大建築事務所と違って，ここには建物分野別のスペシャリストはいない．オバタがあらゆるプロジェクトを統括している．組織論によれば，組織とは個人によって作られた社会的構造であり，特定の共通した目標に向かっての協同体制による追求のために作られている，と言われる．オバタは，こうした社会構造や協同体制を建築家としての自らのなかに作りあげようとしている．彼は流行のスタイルや時代の傾向に影響されることはない．建築のスタイルからすれば，HOKの作品はモダニズムから外れることはない．木造にせよ，煉瓦やタイルを貼ったものにせよ，あるいはガラスと金属の被覆のものにせよ，その形態はいかなるスタイルも装ってはいない．現代の素材が現代の工法によって適材適所の建築を作っている．オバタは建築家としての個性を建築の形態やスタイルを通して表現するのではなく，建築の設計から実現への過程のあり方やすすめ方を通して表現しようとしているのである．時としてHOKの建築にスタイルが欠けていることを咎めるものがいる．だが彼らがHOKの作品を注意深く観察するならば，そこにはスタイルや形態にとらわれない設計理念が一貫していることを認めるだろう．

ギョー・オバタは自らをピープル・オリエンティッドの建築家だと言う．建物は人々の動きに沿って作られなければならないと言う．たとえば，ザ・ガレリアを見るがいい．また，ダラス・フォート・ワース空港を見るがいい．ワシントン D.C. の国立航空宇宙博物館を見るがいい．これらはいずれも人々の動きにたいする細心の研究がなければ成功しなかったものである．水平方向の動きだけではない．垂直方向の動きにたいしても同様に細密な関心が払われる．その結果が高層オフィス・ビルである．HOKの建築を見ると，こうした人々の動きにたいする関心が二つの基本的プランとなって現れている．発展型と凝縮型である．そしてこの二つはあきらかに水平方向と垂直方向の人々の動きに対応しているだろう．

オバタのピープル・オリエンティッドという関心は建築の公共性にたいする関心だと言うこともできよう．それは建物のたんに公共的意義ということではない．17世紀の昔，ヘンリー・ウォットンが要請した便利さと堅固さと楽しさという要素すべてを備えなければ目に見えるようにはならない建物の特質だと言えよう．建築はそれ自体公器であるとする認識をオバタは持っている．だから，彼はうつろいやすい流行や傾向には影響されることはない．装飾や過剰にも関係がない．人々が何を要求しているのか，彼らはどのように動くのか，彼らは何に反応するのか，に答えるべく，オバタはHOKのすべての組織と一体になっているのである．

Statement

Gyo Obata

ステイトメント
ギョー・オバタ

In the 20th century, and especially over the last 40 years, the scale and scope of architectural practice has increased significantly. This has presented architects and other design professionals with increased responsibility and powers, while, at the same time, confronting us with difficult challenges.

The most obvious of these challenges rests simply in the complexity of the projects we now design. Large buildings have become more commonplace and their programs more demanding. We have become accustomed to designing mixed-use centers and corporate headquarters organized as campuses, just as we often are called on to design specialized structures that house sophisticated technology, such as research centers or hospitals.

As projects have grown more complex, so have the demands on the skills and expertise of those responsible for a building's design. In response, we have developed new modes of practice. One example is the large architectural firm that encompasses many disciplines and has offices that stretch around the world. Another is our ability to harness the power of the computer to the many tasks that architecture and design require.

Some architects have responded to the challenges of contemporary practice by becoming more specialized, restricting themselves to certain kinds of projects, or only certain roles within projects. In some cases, well-known architects design only facades, their work derived from styles of architecure concerned for the most part with decoration and not substance. This is not my preference.

I do not believe that size or complexity has to diminish the human side of the architect's work. For me, the architect's work still is a question of essentials, of very basic concerns. Before beginning any project, I want to know as much as I can about the client and his needs and expectations. Then I ask what programmatic considerations need to be met by a thorough and indepth research effort.

Next, I study the site to see what possibilities are naturally available. Now, I want to imagine how people and vehicles and services will flow through the space we have available to us. And, finally, I am curious to see how natural light can be captured and used to enhance the space we will design.

Since I often work quickly and intuitively, my first task always is to understand the project I am working on as a whole, to bring all the human, technological, and design considerations that affect each project into a single focus. And in this, I try never to impose preconceptions, but always to let the project tell me which is the best course to follow.

Like the projects on which I work, I too am the product of many influences. I am a Japanese-American, raised in California and living for most of my life in St. Louis. I have known since I was six years old that I wanted to be an architect, and received strong support in that direction from my family. Since both my parents were artists, our home was very much like a studio all the time, filled with paintings and flowers.

And each of my parents had a special perspective—my father for the world of nature and my mother for the cultures of other people—that has stayed with me. They were both great teachers and taught me life's most basic lesson: to learn to listen very carefully.

When I was six, I spent a year in Japan and remember clearly my grandmother's house, with its remarkable feeling of privacy and serenity. I can still see the beautiful shoji screens and tatami mats throughout, and the guest room in the back that opened on a simple, elegant garden. Everything about that house seemed in its place and in proper proportion. I remember it clearly even now.

At Cranbrook Academy, Eliel Saarinen's teachings also had an enormous influence on me. He emphasized the relationship of every element in a design and the importance of integrating them, from the smallest through the largest. Since then, I have always been interested in working on large-scale projects where many smaller parts must fit within the greater whole. From Saarinen, I learned my most valuable lesson as an architect: always look at the next relationship.

I was influenced as a young architect, as we all were, by the great idols of Modernism: Frank Lloyd Wright, Mies van der Rohe, Corbussier, and Walter Gropius, who taught at Harvard when

Saarinen was at Cranbrook. And I later developed an appreciation for architects with a different approach: Alvar Aalto, who spent some time with us at Cranbrook; Carlo Scarpa in Italy with his imaginative use of materials; and, of course, Louis Sullivan, with his beautifully detailed buildings.

A functional view of the architect's work really is the foundation of my approach to design. Design has meaning for me primarily within the context of the project. I'm interested in a useful design, one that will serve the client and the project without calling attention to itself, one that evolves from the inside out.

How well a building fulfills its human purpose is the standard by which I judge whether that building has meaning. In that way, I am stubbornly pragmatic. Is the completed project a good place in which to live and work? Does it benefit its community? Does it make a positive contribution to its environment? These are the questions I feel we should be asking.

I also believe that architects have a tremendous responsibility in our role as problem-solvers. As our reach increases, as the computer makes us stronger, and our vision stretches around the world, we should remember there are social problems, especially among the homeless and in Third World countries, that might benefit from the application of our more powerful tools and from the use of our increased resources.

In architecture, with each new problem to solve comes a puzzle, with many pieces and many clues to where the pieces fit. If I, like a good detective, learn to read these clues correctly, hopefully I can solve the puzzle. And this gives me great pleasure. I hope always to be involved in solving the puzzles of architecture because, for me, each new problem, each new project, is a kind of rebirth, a way of starting at the beginning and rediscovering the basic functions of architecture.

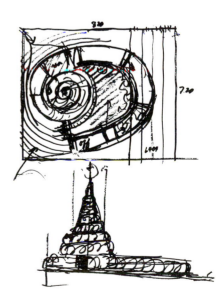

(above) Sketches of the Temple for the Reorganized Church of Jesus Christ of Latter Day Saints.

（上）末日聖徒イエス・キリスト改革教会教会堂スケッチ.

今世紀，特にここ四十数年来，建築実務の規模と範囲は拡大の一途をたどってきた．こうした状況は建築家やデザイナーのもつ責任と権限をより強めてきたと同時に，われわれをして，ますます容易ならぬ試練に直面させる結果となっている．現在手がけているプロジェクトのもつ複雑性の中に，そうした試練の最も明白な例を見ることができる．建物の規模はますます大きくなる傾向にあり，同時にそのプログラムも複雑化している．仕事の内容も，複合的機能をもったセンターや，大学のキャンパスのように様々な分野を集めた企業の本社ビルなどが増え，研究所や病院のように高度なテクノロジーを内包した特別な建物を依頼されることも少なくない．

このようにプロジェクトが複雑化するに伴って，建築を設計する者に求められる専門的知識や技術的熟練のレヴェルもますます高度になってきている．こうした状況に対応するために，私たちは新しい実務形態を模索してきた．その一つが，たくさんのセクションを設け，世界中にオフィス網を拡げる大規模建築設計事務所という形態であり，もう一つが，建築設計やデザインに関わる数多くの作業にコンピュータを利用するという方法である．

何人かの建築家は，今日的な実務の試練に対応するために，ある種のプロジェクトだけを専門的に行うというように分野を制限したり，ひどい場合になると，ある有名建築家のようにファサードしかデザインしなくなるのだが，そのような仕事は単なるデコレーションに過ぎず，建築の本質とはかけ離れたものといえる．こういった方法は私の好むところではない．

私はまた，規模や複雑性の増大が，建築の仕事における人間的な側面を矮小化するものだとは思っていない．私にとって建築の設計とは，常に本質的なものへの問いであり，最も根本的な問題への取り組みである．私はいつもプロジェクトを進める前に，まずできる限りクライアントと彼の必要とし求めるところを理解しようと努め，その後どのようなプログラムを組み立てるべきかを徹底的かつ広範囲なリサーチを行うことによって検討している．

その次に初めて敷地を見て，その土地が本来もっている可能性について研究する．その際に，人や自動車やサーヴィスなどの流れをどうすれば最も効率よく処理できるかということを念頭におかねばならない．そして最後に問題となるのが光である．デザインする空間性を高めるために，自然光をどのように捉え，利用すべきかを考えるのである．

仕事を進めるスピードが速くなり，直観的な判断を必要とする場合が多くなってくるにつれて，目下のプロジェクトの全体を間違いなく把握することが，まず私が最初にすべき重要な仕事となってきた．つまり，それぞれのプロジェクトに関わる人間的な課題や技術的な問題，そしてデザインの方針などといった事柄すべてを，一つの焦点に絞り込んで考えることが必要となってくるのである．このとき大切なことは，できる限り先入観を排して，プロジェクト自体がその進むべき道を私に語ってくれるのに耳を傾けようと努めることである．

私の手になる作品と同じように，私という人間もまた多くの影響のもとに形成された一つの所産であると見ることができよう．私は日系アメリカ人としてカリフォルニアで育ち，その後セントルイスに移って人生の大半をここで過ごしてきた．両親は二人とも芸術家で，6歳の頃にすでに建築家にあこがれていた私を力強く支えてくれた．家庭の雰囲気はまるでアトリエか何かのようで，いつでも絵画や花であふれていた．

父と母はそれぞれ独特の視野をもっていた．父は自然の世界に興味をもち，母は人間のつくり出す文化に関心をもっていた．それらは子供の私に受けつがれている．そんな両親は二人とも偉大な教師であり，私に人生において最も基本となる教えを与えてくれたが，それは，注意深く耳を傾けることを覚えなさい，というものであった．

私が6歳のとき，一年ほど日本の祖母の家で暮らしたことがあった．このとき見た祖母の家は幼い私に強い印象を与え，今でもはっきりと思い出すことができる．周辺のざわめきから隔てられてひっそりとした佇いを見せるその家は，床には畳が敷きつめられ，窓には障子が立てられていた．裏庭に離れの客間があって，簡潔でそれでいて優雅な庭園に向けて開かれていた．建物のあらゆる部分が端正なプロポーションをもち，適切に配されていた．

クランブルック・アカデミーでは，私はエリエル・サーリネンのもとで建築を学んだ．彼がいつもいっていたのは，物と物との関係が大事だということである．小さな物から大きな物まで，デザインにおけるあらゆる要素の相互関係と，それらを統合することの重要性をサーリネンは説いていた．以来私は，たくさんの小さな要素を大きな全体の中で，互いに巧妙に結び付けることが求められるような大規模プロジェクトに興味をもちつづけてきた．こうして私はサーリネンから，建築家としての最も大切なことを学んだのである．つまり，常に隣との関係に目を向けよ，ということである．

そしてまだ駆出しの建築家だった時分，そのころの誰もがそうであったように，私も偉大なるモダニズムの英雄たちの影響を受けていた．フランク・ロイド・ライト，ミース・ファン・デル・ローエ，コルビュジエ，そしてワルター・グロピウス．グロピウスはサーリネンがクランブルックにいた当時，ハーヴァードで教鞭を執っていた．そして彼ら以外にも，その後にそれぞれ異なるアプローチの仕方によって，多くの建築家に学んだ．アルヴァ・アアルトもクランブルックにきたことがあったし，イタリアではカルロ・スカルパの想像力豊かな材料の用い方に触れた．そして，もちろんルイス・サリヴァンの美しいディテールをもった建築からは多くを学んだのだった．

建築家の仕事における機能的な視点というものが，私のデザインの出発点となっている．私は基本的にプロジェクトのもつコンテクストの中にデザインの意味を見出す．私が興味をもっているのは有用なデザインであり，それは一つには，それ自体目立つことなくクライアントやプロジェクトのための役に立つようなという意味であり，一つには内部から外部に向かって発展していくようなものであるといえるだろう．

私にとって，その建物が意味あるものかどうかという判断の基準は，それがいかによく人間の目的にかなっているかどうか，というところにある．その意味において私は頑固にプラグマティックであるといえるだろう．この建物は生活したり働いたりするのにふさわしい場所になりえただろうか？　コミュニティにとって有益だろうか？　周囲の環境に積極的に寄与しているだろうか？　私たちは常に自分自身にこう問いかけなければならないだろう．私はまた，建築家は問題解決者として，きわめて重大な責任を負っていると信じている．私たちの仕事の範囲が拡大し，コンピュータが強力な助っ人になり，そして私たちのヴィジョンがますます国際的なものとなってきた今日，決して忘れてはならないのは，世の中には多くの社会問題が山積しているということである．ホームレスの人たちの問題，あるいは第三世界における問題など，私たちのもつ優れた技術や豊かになった経済力などを上手に活用することによって事態を改善できる問題が少なくない．

もちろん建築の中にも新しい問題がまるでパズルのようにばらまかれている．有能な探偵のようにひとつひとつの手がかりを正しく分析できるなら，私はそのパズルをみごとに解くことができるだろう．私にとってこれ以上の喜びはない．私は常にそんな建築のパズルに取り組んでいきたい．なぜなら，私にとってそういった新しい問題，新しいプロジェクトに対面することは一種の生まれ変わりであり，スタートの位置に着くことであり，建築の基本的な機能を再発見することにつながるからなのだ． （訳：熊倉洋介）

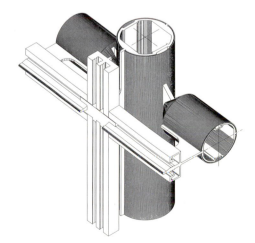

(above) Drawing by CAD: detail of curtain wall retainer rod.
（上）ＣＡＤによるドローイング：カーテン・ウォールの支持ロッド詳細．

Not Stylistic But Attitudinal

George McCue
ギョー・オバタの目指す建築
ジョージ・マッキュー

Although he has placed a large number of buildings in numerous countries for a broad range of uses, Gyo Obata has not endowed his designs with a signature style or vocabulary. His most individual architecture serves only aspectually as prototype for other projects and, like his work generally, transmits no family traits. His stamp on a building is more an authoritative sense of place than a continuity of architectural personality.

Obata's signature is not stylistic but attitudinal. His well-mannered exteriors keep a distance from expressionist statement, arrogance, witticism, emblem, monument, and conversation-piece. Architecture, he has said in various ways, is the outcome of a building design rising to an occasion. Its challenge is to solve problems and bring needs and opportunities into happy coalescence. Architectural style is a manifestation of the spirit in which the challenge is met.

An architect of his time and circumstances, Obata has risen to eminence in an era of massive construction for diverse puroposes. He has served as principal in charge of design since Hellmuth, Obata and Kassabaum, one of the world's largest firms, was founded in St. Louis in 1955. Previously, he had worked for Skidmore, Owings and Merrill in Chicago, where archetypes by Sullivan, Wright, and van der Rohe left imprints on his sense of design and its relatedness to function. In St. Louis, he joined Hellmuth, Yamasaki and Leinweber, which did the thin-shell terminal of the Lambert-St. Louis International Airport. Obata was project architect under designer Minoru Yamasaki, and later would oversee the addition of a fourth bay. In 1955, HYL was dissolved, and George Hellmuth founded HOK with Obata and George E. Kassabaum. Since Hellmuth's retirement in 1978 and the death of Kassabaum in 1982, Obata has been president and chairman.

HOK made itself big to compete for big contracts in its own and other countries. Thus, it moved deliberately into the quicksands of high volume under time and budget pressure, with the consequent vulnerability to expedient design that has given the world stereotyped facades, formula amenities, and interior layouts governed by duct routing. HOK set firm standards for itself, buttressed in all its offices by strong-minded senior designers who operate with considerable autonomy in a structure of oversight checks and balances. Obata generally concentrates on concepts, and is most intensively involved with projects in which problems and possibilities are of critical magnitude. He is a dynamic listener, and in meetings with clients and staff in which words seem to be groping for the point, he defines it with quick, intuitive drawings.

Within the first decade, Obata, then in his thirties, designed more than 90 buildings and complexes in a broad range of types that made known his ready grasp of concept and construction disciplines. They included master plans and buildings for university campuses in Illinois and Trinidad, the U.S. Embassy in San Salvador, and, in St. Louis, the Planetarium, several downtown office structures, the Children's Zoo, and the suburban Priory Church. At the other end of the social-purpose spectrum, is the federal maximum-security prison in Illinois that succeeded Alcatraz in San Francisco Bay.

The circular Priory Church, dominant unit of the Benedictine Priory and School of St. Mary and St. Louis, rises in three ruffles of paraboloid concrete shells, a pristine white blossom placed on the highest level of the 130-acre campus. Twenty arches at the base accommodate side altars and entrances; the middle set defines and admits light to the nave, and the third element functions as the lantern above the high altar.

Soon to be under construction, the Temple for the Reorganized Church of Jesus Christ of Latter Day Saints at Independence, Missouri, takes its form from a sea shell with an extended volute. This becomes the stainless steel clad spire, peaking at 103 meters (340 feet), with a band of clear glass following the upward spiral. These churches and the hyperboloid Planetarium in St. Louis are among Obata's few buildings reading from all sides in the character of sculptured objects.

To a high degree, Obata's buildings invite exploration and give pleasure in work or visitation. The occupants of big architecture constitute substantial temporary populations of broad diversity, and interior malls in particular offer the community intermix that for centuries was the domain of urban plazas and marketplaces. In designing for capacious buildings within a variety of cultural traditions, Obata has maintained a focus on human scale to make high densities tolerable and useful.

The HOK conversion of the long-vacated 1894 Romanesque St. Louis Union Station and its mammoth train shed into a festive mix of shopping malls, luxury hotel, interior streets, and plaza with a broad lagoon, was the country's largest rehabilitation of a historic building. Its popularity has stimulated remodeling and rebuilding in deteriorated blocks around it, one of the reborn buildings having been done over by HOK, which then moved into it.

Houston's suburban Galleria drew delegates away from an American Institute of Architects convention soon after the public first acclaimed its voluminous skylighted arcade with skating rink at the center of multi-level shopping. Underestimating its potency, sponsors provided only suburban-style surface parking. Two expansions include rooftop and below-grade parking. A larger Galleria for Dallas encompasses a three-level mall 366 meters long (1,200 feet), convention facility, integrated parking, and skyline punctuation by three towers—hotel and offices—under vaulted roofs cascading to lower levels.

The Moscone Convention Center, required to go underground in crowded San Francisco, is one of the world's largest column-free exhibition spaces. Its brawny post-tensioned concrete arches, exuberantly high-tech romantic, span 84 meters (275 feet), and support a rooftop park. Obata drew the earlier Cervantes Convention Center in St. Louis with a space-frame roof for huge unimpeded floor space, and cantilevered it commandingly out over the sidewalks. But steel prices caused its sponsors to order it cut back and partitioned. *Post-Dispatch* critic E. F. Porter, Jr., remarked that the submarine pens at Peenemunde were visually more exciting than the result. HOK is now enlarging it.

Presentiments of form may propose themselves in early design stages, but in adherence to the Louis Sullivan precept of function first, Obata begins with use priorities. Then he projects himself into the two-dimensional studies for a mind's-eye tour from space to space to envision three-dimensional experiences within the movement system. The resolved interior determines exterior configuration and finish—opposite the still honored practice of choosing a voguish envelope and stuffing the uses and circulation into it.

His management of voluminous circulation is attested by the National Air and Space Museum in Washington, D.C., with its orderly flow of up to 60,000 daily visitors. Historic flying vehicles are floor-mounted or suspended from tubular trusses within three glass-walled halls of flight, and freestanding staircases to viewing positions at various heights add to the excitement of close inspection. Four alternating marble-faced bays house exhibits and two auditoriums. Concourses on two levels run the museum's full length, 209 meters (685 feet) overall, and visitors are guided to tributary attractions by adroit graphics.

The museum was a rigorous test of Obata's resourcefulness and the firm's resiliency. It was commissioned in 1964 with a $40 million budget. The assigned location was on the Mall, a mile-long (1,609 meters) formal parkway between the Capitol and the Washington Monument, flanked by eclectic architecture; hangar-scale Air/Space was to face the classical National Gallery of Art. Funding was delayed until 1971, but the 1964 budget remained. A revised design that reduced space by 25 percent was rejected by the Fine Arts Commission on points of harmony with other Mall buildings, particularly in its projecting, heavily framed glass elements and a cap overhang with small windows. Obata again redrew the design— seven symmetrically austere elements that alternate void and solid, glass and marble, glazed units set back, marble of the gallery units matching the National Gallery. With phased construction, the museum was finished according to HOK canon—on time and within the budget.

Obata's fluency with intricate concepts, the ability of his teams to keep their heads during ordeals that beset bold enterprises, and the firm's capacity for working with other principals were prominently certified by the Dallas/Fort Worth International Airport, midway between the two competitive cities. It was a joint venture with Brodsky, Hopf and Adler, New York. Semi-circular terminals for 18

big jets or 24 smaller planes, like multiple small airports, are spaced along 6,436 meters (four miles) of an expressway spine, so that travelers have short walks from parking within each loop to the boarding gate. Separate terminals and runways serve specialized operations. At ground level, the architecture is a systematic sequence of handsomely joined precast concrete structures, but the sense of its gargantuan simplicity is perceivable only from the air.

Closely following D/FW in the early 1970s, Obata was plunged into two vast projects in the desert near Riyadh, capital of Saudi Arabia, each a testimonial to formidable management skills. For the King Khalid International Airport, the world's largest at 225 square kilometers (87 square miles), projected for 20 million passengers a year, he created a shimmering vision of geometric Islamic forms. Four public terminals, with space for more, are roofed with gently curved triangular sections in six tiers that rise to 33 meters (108 feet) above the concourses, the sun's glare muted by triangular clerestory openings. Central elements are the royal terminal and an octagonal mosque for 5,000 worshipers within a plaza for 4,000 more, built over a parking garage. Fountains and thousands of irrigated trees make KKIA an oasis in the harsh terrain. Everything that caused all this to rise from the sand was stupefyingly complex— materials and structural components from several countries, concrete, asphalt, and rock-crushing batch plants built on the site, labor force housed in a temporary community of 10,000, a permanent village for personnel of 3,000. The governing concept: a magnificent gateway to the kingdom and a memorable experience for passengers, who were to feel no uncertainties about where they were and where they were going, no matter which of the 80 escalators and elevators they might be using.

The other is King Saud University, its campus nine square. kilometers (3.5 square miles), to accommodate 20,000 students, built in less than 40 months, the cost $4 billion. An architectural-engineering consortium, HOK+4, won the commission, Obata as design principal with Gollins, Melvin, Ward of London. Ten colleges and support facilities are grouped along walkways extended from three main spines. Utility lines are beneath the walkways, and there is space for internal transportation beneath the spines. The colonnaded walkways converge on a seven-story forum paved with granite mosaics, adjacent to the administration building, a two-million-volume library, and a theater building. Two years of design work produced 6,000 sheets of working drawings and 10,000 sheets of specifications for construction of 621,000 square meters (6.7 million square feet) of buildings by craftsmen of 23 nationalities speaking 16 languages. Under a fixed-price construction agreement insisted on by Saudi Arabia, the university was completed on schedule.

Obata owns most of the skyline of downtown St. Louis, his home city. Two of his early towers, Boatmen's Bank and the Equitable Building, just west of Eero Saarinen's Gateway Arch on blocks flanking the historic Old Courthouse, make gestures of urbane gentility. Obata pulled back the towers back, with extensions on the Courthouse sides held to the height of its cornice. His third recent tower is Metropolitan Square, 42 stories of gold-bronze granite and glass. The pitched copper roof of its glassed penthouse echoes the French second-empire summit of a tall hospital in the same expressway view, and oriels respond to the light-and-shadow texture of the nearby Chemical Building, a landmark inspired by Chicago's Tacoma Building. The sidewalks are arcaded, and 1,000 automobiles can be parked internally.

Between two Cleveland landmarks, Obata placed the BP America tower so as to extend its low glass-front, step-walled garden entrance toward the plaza faced on the other side by the Terminal Tower, and to connect with the much-loved Old Arcade via a lofty interior gallery. In Pittsburgh's riverfront Golden Triangle, an enclave of corporate headquarters, One Oxford Centre—four octagonal shafts on a central axis, 46 stories—presents a faceted composition in reflective glass and silvery aluminum. Obata favors light coloristic effects in his towers.

Some companies dislike towers. Levi Strauss, makers of jeans since the California gold rush, tried high-rise and soon missed the unstratified relationships of its former low but crowded headquarters in San Francisco. HOK designed a complex of three new buildings

and a rehabilitated warehouse—the tallest seven stories—in bayfront
street scale. Setbacks of the red brick walls (in precast panels as an
earthquake precaution) continue the rhythms of terraced houses on
steep Telegraph Hill. Another touch of color is both ingratiating and
promotional—trusses of the glassed entrance lobby were painted
denim blue. Landscape architect Lawrence Halprin converted
remaining ground space into a public plaza and park with a little
stream and fountain structures of cut stone and Sierra Nevada rock.
A familiar charactrization of HOK projects, "the world's largest,"
applies to the St. Louis computer center for the McDonnell Douglass
Information Systems Group, which has programmed and guided
flights for the National Aeronautic and Space Administration besides
its own design work for aircraft and space vehicles. The
nine-building complex occupies more than a million square feet, of
which computer facilities use 25,548 square meters (275,000 square
feet). Ducts the height of the computer center remove excess heat,
four times enough to warm the complex on the coldest days. In
sleek profile, metal skin, emphatic color panels, and long interior
perspectives, the group is decisively but not obsessively high-tech. An
increasingly significant design consideration was to make the
buildings architecturally readable from expressway automobiles. The
first seven were designed and built in 24 months.
Computer-assisted design systems, with software by in-house
architect-programmers, have become major HOK tools from
schematics to the bidding process and facilities management.
Networking its main offices has contributed, says vice chairman
Jerome Sincoff, to "much more communication and coordination
between disciplines that promote a real team spirit." The software is
being marketed by an HOK spinoff company.
CAD systems and the multidisciplinary approach had broad
application in the Kellogg Company Headquarters at Battle Creek,
Michigan. The manufacturer of cereal foods proposed a remarkable
collaboration—the city to create a more positive business climate by
annexing an adjoining township, the company to purchase a blighted
former industrial site of six hectares (15 acres) and help fund
comprehensive planning to assert new identify as a town center. The
site included a park and a stretch of the Battle Creek River, both
neglected as urban assets. HOK was commissioned to design the
Kellogg building, in which Obata became directly involved, and do
the town-center planning.
All the participating disciplines—architects, engineers, landscape
designers, interior designers, and art and graphics personnel—were
moved into a separate suite of the St. Louis offices for close
interaction. The Facility Programming Group's computers developed
charts of growth patterns and lines of communication that clarified
immediate and future needs. The outcome was a well-defined city
center with Kellogg as a principal anchor in a headquarters that
speaks for its personal management style. The five-story building is
two mirror-image units in red brick with setbacks and rounded
corners in the spirit of the Levi Strauss group, with a connecting
atrium. Design elements take note of architecture by Louis Sullivan,
Frank Lloyd Wright, and Eliel Saarinen in that region, and interior
spaces are enhanced with art works.
The ability of HOK to apply a broad range of services to large,
intricate problems accounts for much of its success in bringing
projects of unusual complexity to completion on time and within the
budget; Obata's design sense has put well-working buildings of
landmark quality on several continents and held the allegiance of his
clients.

George McCue

George McCue was born in
Lipscomb, Texas, in 1910. After
graduation from the University
of Missouri School of
Journalism, Columbia, he was
reporter and editor on several
Missouri newspapers and the
Associated Press. From 1943
until retirement in 1975 he was
a staff member of the *St. Louis
Post-Dispatch*, the last nineteen
years as art and urban design
critic. He is the author of three
editions of *The St. Louis
Building Art: Two Centuries*, an
architectural guide published by
the St. Louis Chapter, American
Institute of Architects, and
co-author of the 1989 revision,
*A Guide to the Architecture of
St. Louis*. He also is the author
of *Sculpture City: St. Louis,
Public Sculpture and Statuary in
the "Gateway to the West."*
1988, sponsored by Laumeier
Sculpture Park. He is an
honorary member of the
American Institute of Architects.

ギョー・オバタはこれまでに数多くの国々で，幅広い用途にわたる建築を手がけてきたが，彼の作品には固定したスタイルやボキャブラリーというものは与えられていない．彼が特に個人的にデザインした建築が，単に外観上，他のプロジェクトにたいするプロトタイプとなることはあっても，ある種の内輪的な特性を与えるようなことはなかった．彼の建物に見られる特徴は，一貫した建築的固有性というよりも，厳然たる場所の感覚に基づいたものなのである．つまり「オバタらしさ」とは，スタイルではなく，態度なのだ．彼のつくる建物のスマートな外観は，表現主義的な主張や傲慢さ，ジョーク，象徴性や記念性，あるいは目立たせるためのデザインなどとは，はっきりと距離をおいたものである．彼はいう，「建築とは，場合に応じてデザインした結果現れてくるものである」，と．そしてそこでの試練が，問題を解決し，要求を拾いあげ，最善の方策をもって幸ある統合をなしとげることなのである．建築のスタイルとは，この試練と向かい合う精神の現れなのだ．

オバタと同じ世代，あるいは同じような環境をもつ他の建築家たちと比べてみても，彼は多様な目的をもつ大規模建築の時代における，一つの卓越した存在であるといえよう．現在，世界で最も大きな事務所の一つとなったヘルムース・オバタ・アンド・カサバウム（HOK）を1955年にセントルイスで創立して以来，彼は常にデザインを預かる責任者として活躍してきた．

それ以前，彼はシカゴの SOM で働いていたが，ここでの経験が，彼のデザイン・センスや機能にたいする考え方などの原型を，サリヴァン，ライト，そしてミースに見出すことのできる一因となっている．その後セントルイスに移ったオバタは，薄シェル構造のランバート・セントルイス空港のターミナルで知られるヘルムース・ヤマサキ・アンド・レインウェーバー事務所（HYL）に入る．ここで彼はミノル・ヤマサキの下でプロジェクト・アーキテクトを務め，のちに空港の増築を監理する．1955年に HYL が解散すると，ジョージ・ヘルムースはオバタ，ジョージ・E・カサバウムとともに HOK を創設する．そして1978年にヘルムースが引退し，1982年にカサバウムが亡くなると，オバタが社長となった．

HOK は国内外における膨大な契約に対応するために，その組織を拡大していった．その結果，時間と予算のプレッシャーのもとで，徐々に肥満体質の弊害を招いてゆき，画一的なファサード，標準型の設備，そしてダクト配置によって決定される内部のレイアウトといった御都合主義のデザインを行うようになり，必然的に建物の質は低下していった．そこで HOK は全社的な基準を設定するとともに，高い意識をもった上級デザイナーにかなりの自律性を与えて，業務の管理にあたらせるシステムを採用した．そしてオバタ自身はおもにコンセプトづくりに専念し，特に問題があり可能性の点で重要性をもつプロジェクトにのみ，集中的に関わるといった方法をとるようになった．彼は精力的な聞き手で，クライアントやスタッフなどとのミーティングの場において，議論がポイントをとらえようとしていると，すばやく直観的なスケッチによってそれを示して見せるのである．

HOK の最初の10年間に，30代だったオバタは90以上もの様々なタイプのビルやコンプレックスを設計したが，そうした中で，すばやくコンセプトを捕える能力や建設のためのノウハウなどを培っていった．その頃の作品としては，イリノイとトリニダードでのキャンパスのマスター・プランと建物の計画，サン・サルヴァドルのアメリカ大使館，セントルイスのプラネタリウム，いくつかの市庁舎，子供用動物園，郊外の小修道院などがある．また，同じく公共建築でも変わったものとしてイリノイの刑務所があるが，これはサンフランシスコ湾のアルカトラズ刑務所に次いでアメリカで最大級の保安警備を誇るものである．また，セントルイスおよびセントマリー地区のベネディクト会修道院の本部である円形の教会建築を設計しているが，これは HP シェルの3段のひだによる造型が，あたかも130エーカーのキャンパスの丘に咲く，可憐な白い花のようである．基部には20のアーチが連なっており，小さな聖壇とエントランスになっている．その上段壁面には外陣に自然光を導くための窓が開けられており，最上階の部分は聖壇上部の明かり採りとなっている．

ミズーリ州インディペンデンスの末日聖徒イエス・キリスト改革教会の教会堂は，まもなく建設にとりかかるだろうが，渦巻き貝に由来する独特の形態をしている．これは高さ103メートルのステンレスの尖塔で，ガラスの連窓が螺旋状に巡っている．これらの教会建築やセントルイスの双曲線形のプラネタリウムは，オバタの作品の中でも，外観全体を彫塑的にまとめた数少ない例である．オフィス・ビルのような建築を例にあげると，オバタの手になるビルはそこを訪れる人々や働く人々に喜びを与え，楽しんで中を歩き回れるような建物が多い．大きなビルを利用する人間は，一時的にはかなりの数になり，しかも多様な個性をもって集まってくる．そのため，特にビル内部のモールなどは，かつては都市の広場や市場が担っていたようなコミュニティの交流の場になっているといえるだろう．様々な文化的伝統の中でこのような大きなビルをデザインする場合，オバタは常にヒューマン・スケールを大切にしてきた．それが建物に，優れた使いやすさと快適性を与えることができた理由である．

HOK によるセントルイス・ユニオン・ステーションの再開発計画は，アメリカにおける最も大規模な，歴史的建造物の再生プロジェクトだった．それは，長い間放置されたままだった1894年に建ったロマネスクの駅舎とその巨大な列車庫を，ショッピング・モール，高級ホテル，アーケード，そして大きな池のある広場などを組み合せた一大複合建築として甦らせようというものであった．そしてこの施設の人気が周囲の荒廃していたブロックに刺激を与え，これを機会に改造，改築を行う建物が増えていった．

ヒューストン郊外に設計した商業施設，ガレリアをまず最初に評価したのは一般の市民たちだった．大きなガラス天井で覆われたアーケードと中心にスケート・リンクをもつ，多層のショッピング・センターが周辺の評判になると，すぐに A.I.A. の代表がやってきた．ところがその魅力を過小評価していたスポンサーは，当初簡単な青天井の駐車場しか用意していなかったので，2度の増築によってやっと屋根つきの駐車場が準備される始末だった．また，これより大きなガレリアがダラスにつくられている．長さ366メートルに及び3層のショッピング・モールに集会室や機能的な駐車場，そしてスカイラインのポイントとなる3本のタワー――ホテルとオフィスが入っている――をもつ施設がヴォールト天井の下に広がっている．

建物の密集するサンフランシスコの街の地下に計画されたモスコーン・コンヴェンション・センターは，無柱空間としては世界で最も広いエキジビション・センターの一つである．スパン84メートルの雄大なポスト・テンション・コンクリートのアーチは，まさに，華麗なるハイ・テク・ロマンと呼べるもので，それは地上の屋上公園を支えている．また，セントルイスのセルヴァンテス・コンヴェンション・センターの初期の計画案では，スペース・フレームによる大屋根が広大な無柱空間を覆い，そのままカンティレヴァーで外側に張り出して，歩道の上に力強い庇を形づくっていた．しかし，鉄材のコスト高を理由にスポンサーが規模の縮小と空間の間仕切りを命じたため，オバタの描いたこの初期案はお蔵入りとなってしまった．ところが『ポスト・ディスパッチ』紙の批評家，E・F・ポーターJr. がこの初期案のドローイングを取りあげ，建設された縮小案よりも視覚的にはるかにエキサイティングだと評価した．その結果，HOK は現在その拡張工事に入っている．

デザインの初期の段階では，一般的にいってまず形態から発想する場合が多いが，サリヴァンの機能優先の考え方に順ずるオバタは，まず使い勝手の面からアプローチしてゆく．それから図面上でのスタディに入ってゆくわけだが，ここでは動線システムの中で，空間から空間へ移動するときの3次元的な空間体験を心の目によって想い描きながらスタディを進めてゆく．このようにして導き出された内部空間が，外観の形状と仕上げを決定してゆくのである．こうした設計の進め方は，いまだにもてはやされている，最初に流行のスタイルでパッケージをつくってしまい，そこに機能や動線をつめ込むといった方法とは，まったく正反対のものである．

複雑な動線の処理における彼の優れた能力は，ワシントン D.C. に建設された国立航空宇宙博物館によって証明されよう．ここでは一日平均6万人を超える来館者を，秩序正しい流れによって処理している．ガラスの壁で囲まれた三つのホールには，歴史的な飛行機が床に固定されたり天井のトラスから吊り下げ

(above) Drawing by CAD: elevation of 801 Grand Avenue.

（上）ＣＡＤによるドローイング：801グランド・アヴェニュー立面図.

られたりして展示されており，ところどころに近寄って見るための独立した階段が設けられていて，様々なレヴェルからの視点が用意されている．それ以外に，４種類の大理石貼りの展示スペースとオーディトリアムなどがあり，博物館全体を貫く２層のコンコースは長さ209メートルになる．人々はパネルやアトラクションによって展示の説明を受けながらここを進んでゆく．

だがこの博物館の建設は，オバタの才腕と組織の柔軟性に対する厳しい試練であったのだ．1964年に結ばれた契約では，予算は4,000万ドルで，敷地は国会議事堂とワシントン・モニュメントを結ぶ１マイルの，折衷主義の建築が建ち並ぶ，モールと呼ばれる格式のあるパーク・ウェイに沿った場所であった．ここには向かい側に古典的なナショナル・ギャラリーが建っていた．契約はしたものの，予算がおりるのが1971年まで遅れ，しかも1964年に決められた額はそのままだった．そこで設計を変更し，規模を25%縮小した案を提出すると，こんどは芸術協会がこの案に反対した．理由は他のモールにある建物と調和しないというもので，特に建物から突き出したガラスのフレームと，小さな窓のあいた張り出した屋根が問題にされた．そこでオバタはふたたびデザインを練り直し，七つの左右対称の禁欲的な要素が並ぶ案をまとめた．これは，ヴォイドとソリッド，ガラスと大理石が交互に組み合され，ガラスのユニットがセットバックし，そして展示棟の大理石がナショナル・ギャラリーとうまくマッチした案であった．何期かにわたる工事の末，完成した博物館は，果たしてHOKの規律──工期と予算の厳守──に従うものであった．

オバタの難解なコンセプトを説明する流暢さと，大胆な冒険を阻む障害に冷静に対処する彼の部下たちの有能さ，そして他の事務所との協同をこなす組織の柔軟性を十分に示して見せたのが，二つの競合する街の中間に建設された，ダラス/フォートワース国際空港の計画である．この仕事は，ニューヨークのブロドスキィ・ホフ・アンド・アドラーとの協同によるものであった．大型ジェット機18機，あるいは小型機24機のための半円型のターミナル群は，小さな空港を集めたように，背骨となる6436メートル（４マイル）の長さの高速道路に沿って一定の間隔で配置されている．そのため乗客は駐車場から各搭乗ゲートへ短い距離を歩くだけでよい．この分散したターミナルと滑走路は特殊な効果をもっており，地上からはプレキャスト・コンクリート構造による端正でシステマティックな外観しか見ることはできないが，上空から見下ろしたとき初めてその驚くべきシンプルさの意味を認めることができるのである．

ダラス/フォートワース空港につづいてすぐの1970年代の初め，オバタはサウジアラビアの首都リヤド近くの砂漠で，二つのプロジェクトに取り組むことになった．それらはどちらも膨大な作業量を必要とする大がかりな計画であった．その一つ，キング・ハリド国際空港は，世界最大の２万2,500ヘクタールという面積に，年間の搭乗者数が延べ2,000万人というもので，ここで彼は幾何学的なイスラム模様をモティーフにした輝くような光景をつくりだした．四つの一般用ターミナルとその付属のスペースは，ゆるやかな曲線を描きながら立ち上がる段状の屋根に覆われており，33メートルの天井高をもつコンコースの上部にとられた明かり採りからは，まぶしさを抑えた柔らかな光が導き入れられている．施設の中心は王家のためのターミナルと，同時に5,000人の礼拝が可能な八角形のモスクで，さらに4,000人を収容できるプラザとともに，駐車場の上に置かれている．また，噴水と灌漑による何千本もの樹木が，この空港を砂漠の中のオアシスにしている．この計画では，工事を行うために準備された施設だけでも膨大な複合施設であった．世界中から送られてくる様々な材料や構造部品をストックする倉庫，コンクリート，アスファルト，そして砕石のための工場群，さらに１万人の労働者のための仮設の宿舎と，3,000人の従業員が生活できるヴィレッジなどが建てられた．全体を貫くコンセプトは，王国の入口として威厳に満ち，かつ訪問者の思い出に残る雰囲気をもつ建物とすることであり，同時に，利用者にとってわかりやすく，たとえ80基におよぶエレヴェータやエスカレータのどれに乗っても，迷わず目指す場所にたどり着けるような，明快な建物であることが基本であった．

サウジアラビアでのもう一つの仕事がキング・サウド大学の計画である．キャンパスの広さ900ヘクタール，学生数２万人という規模の大学を，工期40ヵ月，予

算40億ドルでつくるというものだった．このプロジェクトは，HOK と他の4社との協同設計であったが，デザイン責任者はオバタが務めた．キャンパスの背骨となる3本の主道からのびた遊歩道に沿って，10のカレッジとその付属施設のグループが配置された．その遊歩道の下には設備用の配管が，そして主道の下には運搬用スペースがとられた．並木のつづく遊歩道は，花崗岩のモザイクで舗装されたフォーラムに集まっており，これに隣接して管理棟，200万冊収蔵の図書館，そして劇場が建てられている．　2年間の設計作業の中で，延床面積62万1,000平方メートルの建物のために6,000枚の実施設計図と1万枚に及ぶ施工図が描かれ，その作業に携わった技術者は23ヵ国，16種類の言葉が飛び交った．こうして，当初決められた予算内で，スケジュール通りに大学は完成した．

セントルイスはオバタの故郷の市であるが，そのダウン・タウンのスカイラインを形づくっている建物の多くが彼の手になるものである．初期の作品である二つのビル，ボートメンズ・バンクとエクイタブル・ビルは，有名なエーロ・サーリネンのゲイトウェイ・アーチのすぐ西側に立っているが，そこはまた，由緒ある旧裁判所に隣接するブロックである．都市的で上品な雰囲気をもったこの二つのビルを，のちに背面の裁判所側に増築したが，どちらも裁判所のコーニスの高さにそろえて新設部分を付け加えた．彼の3番目に新しいメトロポリタン・スクエアは，42階建ての金色あるいはブロンズ色の花崗岩とガラスでできたタワーである．このビルは，シカゴのタコマ・ビルを意識したケミカル・ビルに隣り合って立っており，その屋上のガラスのペントハウスを覆う銅葺き屋根や壁面の出窓は，ケミカル・ビルのフランスの第2帝政風の頂部や陰影のあるテクスチュアと呼応したものになっている．またアーケードになった歩道と1,000台収容できる駐車場を備えている．

クリーヴランドの二つのランドマークであるターミナル・タワーとオールド・アーケードに狭まれて建つ BP アメリカ・タワーでは，ターミナル・タワー側にあるプラザに向かって段状のガーデン・エントランスがのび，反対側では天井の高いギャラリーによってアーケードと結ばれている．

ピッツバーグの河岸のゴールデン・トライアングルと呼ばれる地区に建つワン・オックスフォード・センターは，軸上に並ぶ4本の八角形のシャフトからなる46階建ての本社ビルである．このビルの外観は，ミラー・ガラスと銀色のアルミニウムの2種類の面による構成によっている．オバタはこのような軽い感じの色彩手法を好んで用いている．

クライアントによっては，タワーを好まないところもある．カリフォルニアのゴールド・ラッシュ時代からつづいているジーンズ・メーカー，リーヴァイ・ストラウス社は，サンフランシスコにあった低層の本社ビルが手狭になったので，超高層ビルに会社を移したところ，まもなく以前の上下のへだてのない自由な雰囲気が失われてしまった．そこで HOK がデザインした3つの新しいビルと古い倉庫を改造したコンプレックスは，いちばん高い棟でも7階建てで，湾岸沿いのストリート・スケールに合ったものになっている．セットバックしている赤い煉瓦の外壁（耐震壁のためプレキャスト・パネルとしている）はテレグラフ・ヒルの斜面に並ぶテラス・ハウスのリズムを繰り返している．またもう一つの色使いとしては，ジーンズ・メーカーということで，トラス構造のガラス張りのロビーを，デニム・ブルーに塗っている．そして造園設計家のローレンス・ハルプリンは，残った敷地に，切り石とシェラ・ネバタの岩を使って小川と噴水をつくり，パブリック・プラザと公園に仕立て上げている．

HOK の手がけるプロジェクトに冠されることの多い「世界最大」という表現が，セントルイスのマクドネル・ダグラスのコンピュータ・センターにもつけられている．マクドネル・ダグラス・インフォメーション・システム・グループは，航空機や宇宙船の設計業務の他に，NASA の飛行計画の管理やプログラムづくりなどにも携わっている会社である．その九つのビルからなるコンプレックスは100万平方フィート以上の面積を有し，そのうちの¼以上をコンピュータ用の施設が占めている．このコンピュータ・センター内では，ダクトによって機械の廃熱を回収し，コンプレックス全体の暖房に利用する仕組みになっていて，それだけで最も寒い日に必要となる熱量の4倍ものエネルギーを得ることができるのである．その洗練された外観，メタル・スキン，目を引くカラー・

パネル，そして長大な内部空間など，この会社はまぎれもなく，そして現実的な意味でもハイ・テクであるといえよう．また，近年とみに重視されつつあるデザイン上の課題は，ハイウェイを走る車からの視線に，建物をどう印象づけるかということである．このコンプレックスの最初の7棟は，設計から施工までを24ヵ月で終了した．

HOK 社内のアーキテクト・プログラマーがつくるソフトを用いたコンピュータ・デザイン（CAD）・システムは，製図作業にとどまらず，入札プロセスやファシリティ・マネージメントなどにおいても欠かすことのできない道具となっている．HOK 副社長のジェローム・シンコフは，同社の主要オフィス間のネットワーク効果について，「様々な業務に携わる人間を相互に結び付け，コミュニケーションやコーディネーションを容易にすることが可能になり，それが組織内部のチーム・スピリットをより一層高めている」と語っている．これらのソフトは HOK から販売されている．

ミシガン州バトル・クリークの，コーン・フレークで有名なケロッグ社の本社ビルの計画では，CAD システムと，この部門間のネットワーキングによるアプローチが大幅に取り入れられた．ケロッグ社からの依頼は，市当局との注目すべき協同開発事業であった．荒廃したかつての工業地域の6ヘクタールの土地をケロッグ社が払い受け，資金面の援助をしながら新たなタウン・センターを開発する包括的な計画であり，当局側はこれによって地域の活性化とビジネス街の誕生を期待した．この敷地には公園とバトル・クリーク川からの運河があったが，すでに打ち捨てられたものとなっていた．このケロッグ・ビルの設計には，オバタ自身が直接携わり，タウン・センターの全体計画を含めて，彼の手によって進められた．

すべての部門の関係者──建築家，技術者，造園設計家，インテリア・デザイナー，そして芸術家たち──が緊密なコミュニケーションを図るため，セントルイス事務所の中に設けられた独立したセクションに集合した．そしてファシリティ・プログラム・グループのコンピュータは，現在および将来の要求を明らかにする成長パターンとコミュニケーション・ラインのチャートを打ち出した．こうして今や素晴らしく整備されたシティ・センターとなったこの地区で，ケロッグ社はリーダー的存在であり，その個人経営のスタイルを物語っている．その建物は，二つの左右対称のユニットがアトリウムによって結ばれており，隅部の丸い，セットバックした赤い煉瓦貼りの外観は，リーヴァイ・ストラウス・ビルの精神に通じるものがある．そしてデザイン・エレメントのいくつかは，この地方に建つサリヴァンやライトやエリエル・サーリネンの建築を参照しており，その内部空間は芸術作品によって一層豊かなものになっている．

困難かつ膨大な問題に対する，HOK のもつ広範囲な処理能力の優秀さは，いかなる複雑なプロジェクトといえども，定められた期間内に与えられた予算で確実に完成させてきたという実績によって証明されるだろう．そしてオバタは，その優れたデザイン・センスによって世界中に機能的でランドマーク性の高いビルを実現し，ますます彼のクライアントたちの信頼を高めているのである．

（訳：熊倉洋介）

ジョージ・マッキュー
1910年，テキサス州に生まれる．ミズーリ大学新聞学部を卒業，ミズーリ州の数紙のレポーター，編集の仕事をした．1943年から，1975年に引退するまで，『セントルイス・ポスト・ディスパッチ』紙のスタッフであり，最後の19年間は，芸術や都市デザインの批評を担当した．彼はA.I.A.の名誉会員でもある．

A Look at HOK

設計組織 HOK の有機的な構造

HOK's practice includes a wide range of design disciplines, building types and geographic locations. This diversity helps the firm avoid the economic instability that is traditionally associated with architectural firms dedicated to one design specialty, a limited range of building types, or to a single geographic region.

HOK's commitment to providing design services of the highest caliber, regardless of project size or type, is demonstrated by its practice of employing specialists from many disciplines to bring integrated design to all projects.

However, remaining dedicated to the highest standards of a multidisciplinary design practice, while ensuring the firm's ongoing financial health, often requires a strenuous balancing act. The well-being of the firm requires structure, but too much structure discourages the best creative work. The solution is never simple. As design professionals and administrators, HOK's managers remain committed to the task of creating what one describes as a management structure that is "invisible but effective."

Ranked among the largest design firms in the United States, Hellmuth, Obata & Kassabaum currently employs more than 1,000 people located in ten offices throughout the United States, in Europe and the Pacific Rim. In fiscal year 1989 alone, HOK engaged in projects amounting to $50 million square feet with a total value of $2.5 billion. In a typical week, as many as 350 different projects another are under way throughout HOK's offices.

By most standards, a firm of 1,000 employees is not unusual. But in the field of architectural design services—where only 250 firms in the United States, for instance, employ more than 50 people—the number of employees and design disciplines that make up HOK is exceptional. And while the firm's diversity and size allow it to work on some of the most ambitious and exciting projects in the world, its size and diversity remain a constant managerial challenge.

A division of responsibility has always been inherent in HOK's approach to running an architectural design practice. Those essential skills represented by HOK's three founding members—marketing, design, and project management—remain the cornerstones on which the management of the firm still is based.

But now the Office of the Chairman, the body with primary executive responsibilities with the firm, includes four principals: Chairman and President Gyo Obata, HOK's director of design; Vice Chairman King Graf, in charge of marketing; Vice Chairman Jerome J. Sincoff, responsible for operations and project management; and Vice Chairman Robert E. Stauder, charged with financial and legal responsibilities.

All four members of the Office of the Chairman are graduates of the Washington University School of Architecture in St. Louis, and have been with HOK for the majority of their careers. Having risen through the firm, they understand the inner workings of HOK almost intuitively. Their long-standing relationship with HOK leads them to rely on "people" skills, rather than abstract management theories.

This insistence on a people-oriented approach that emphasizes the highest standards of creative accomplishment—what marketing director King Graf likes to describe as an atmosphere of "serious informality"—distinguishes much of the working environment at HOK. Commitment to a team method of organization assures the concentration of skills required for each project. Clearly identified project goals become the context within which each team member contributes; the respect for creative contributions evident throughout the firm encourages individual initiative.

To HOK's managers, encouraging the conditions for the best creative work goes hand in hand with a client-oriented practice. The goal of "adaptability" that Vice Chairman Sincoff describes as the result of a flexible working environment also translates in HOK terms into a creative process that places primary importance on client and project goals.

To enhance both creative work and clearly focused client relationships, each of HOK's offices is kept to a maximum of 100 to 125 employees. Only the St. Louis office, where 300 firm members are joined by a corporate staff of 50, exceeds this number. Recently, however, the St. Louis office has restructured itself into three separate groups, each concentrating on a specific area of work:

public and institutional facilities, commercial and retail facilities, and corporate facilities. This division allows a greater concentration of capabilities on each project and better service to each client.

"We are very concerned about building a partnership with the client, because we feel that understanding and communication really is the basis of good design," Gyo Obata explains. "The most important work we do often takes place in the minds of the people involved in that project, and in the sharing of ideas."

While the Office of the Chariman remains the focus of administration, in recent years non-design professionals in communications, finance, and human resources have been added to the firm's central management staff. This has resulted in a stronger core structure to support the firm's regional offices which function as a relatively autonomous reflections of the whole.

The importance of relationships that transcend organizational guidelines, very much a part of the firm's culture, continues to be apparent at HOK—even as the firm's increased size demands additional administrative structure. Most formally, it is evident in a board of directors, composed of senior members of the firm, that advises the Office of the Chairman.

The HOK ethic of encouraging creative achievement can also be seen in the informal network of national boards formed to represent the disciplines of design, engineering, planning, and interiors, as well as the areas of marketing and project management. These boards encourage intra-disciplinary dialogue and extend the influence of the team approach, insuring an organization-wide concentration on the creative process.

As the firm continues to grow, it remains committed to diversification of project type, a multidisciplinary approach, and to a thoughtful, client-oriented process that results in good design and client satisfaction. Imbedded in its culture is the recognition that administrative efficiency, in the words of Vice Chairman Stauder, "must be carried out in support of good design. When we concentrate on improving our business practices, it is only as a means to foster greater creativity."

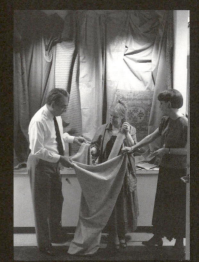

Photos (pp.16-19) by Burt Glinn / Magnum Photos Inc.

HOK の仕事は，設計分野，建物種別，建設地域などにおいて多種多様なものを手がけている．この多様性によって，ある特定の設計分野，限られた種類の建物，あるいはある一つの地域だけを専門とする建築事務所につきものの経営の不安定さを免れている．

プロジェクトの規模や種類にかかわらず，常に最高の設計を行おうという HOK の姿勢は，この事務所があらゆるプロジェクトにおいて完璧な設計をするために多様な分野の専門家を集めていることにも表れている．

しかし，多分野にわたって最高水準の設計業務をつづけていくには，HOK の現在の健全な経営状態を維持すると同時に，しばしば強引な均衡策が必要である．会社の繁栄のためには組織が必要だが，組織が大きすぎると最高の創造的仕事を邪魔することになる．この解決は容易ではない．HOK の経営陣は，ある人が「目に見えない，しかし効果的な」と表現する経営組織を目指して，日々努力をつづけている．

ヘルムース・オバタ・アンド・カサバウム（HOK）は，アメリカで最大規模の設計組織であり，現在，全米，ヨーロッパ，および環太平洋地域の10ヵ所の事務所に，1,000人を超える所員をもつ．1989会計年度だけでも，HOK は計5,000万平方フィート，総額25億ドルのプロジェクトに携った．ある週では350もの異なった新しいプロジェクトが各地の HOK の事務所で進行している．

大方の基準からすれば，従業員1,000人の会社というのは珍しくない．しかし，建築設計の分野では，50人以上の会社は全米でもわずか250社ほどであり，HOK の所員数と設計分野の多様性は例外的な規模といえる．HOK はその多様性と規模の大きさによって世界でも最も野心的で興味深いプロジェクトを手がけることができるが，一方，その規模と多様性のゆえに常に経営管理の難しさがつきまとう．

建築設計の仕事を遂行するやり方として，HOK は常に責任の分担を行ってきた．HOK の3人の創立メンバーがそれぞれ代表する不可欠の技術，すなわちマーケティング，設計，そしてプロジェクト管理，これらが現在でも HOK の経営の基盤となっている．

しかし，現在は，直接的経営責任を有する組織体である会長会は4人の長によって構成されている．すなわち，HOK の設計部門の役員で会長兼社長のギョー・オバタ，マーケティング担当の副会長キング・グラフ，経営およびプロジェクト管理責任の副会長ジェローム・J・シンコフ，そして財政および法務に責任をもつ副会長のロバート・E・スタウダーである．

会長会の4人のメンバーはすべてセントルイスのワシントン大学建築学科を卒業していて，彼らはこれまでの大半を HOK で過ごしている．HOK とともに育ってきた彼らは，HOK の運営をほとんど直観的に理解しており，HOK との長い付き合いの中で，抽象的な経営理論よりもむしろ「人」の技量を頼みにするようになっている．

最高レヴェルの創造的完成に重きをおくこの人材重視の方法へのこだわり——マーケティング責任者のキング・グラフは好んで「形式ばらないが真剣な」雰囲気と呼ぶ——は，HOK のオフィス環境を大きく特徴づけるものである．チーム方式に徹することにより，各プロジェクトに必要な技術の集中を確実にする．プロジェクトの目標を明確にし，チームの各人がそれに向かって貢献する．つまり，事務所全体を通して創造的に貢献するという空気が，個々のイニシアティヴを促進するのである．

HOK の経営陣にとって，創造的な仕事に最適な環境を整えることと，クライアント本位の仕事とは，相互に重なり合うものである．フレキシブルなオフィス環境の成果としてシンコフ副会長が「適合性」の目標と表現するものは，HOK においては，すなわちクライアントとプロジェクトの目標を最優先する創造プロセスとも言い換えられる．

創造的な仕事，そしてクライアントとの明確な関係の両方を推し進めるために，HOK の各事務所は，最大100～125名の人員に抑えている．セントルイス事務所だけは，50名の法人スタッフによって300名の人員となっていて，この数を超えているが，ここも最近3つのグループに再編され，各グループが特定の分野に集中するようになった．すなわち，公共施設，商業施設，および企業施設の3

部門に分かれたのである．この分割によって，各プロジェクトに，より能力を集中できるようになり，クライアントに，よりよいサーヴィスが可能になった．

「私たちは，よい設計の基本は実際のところ理解とコミュニケーションであると実感しているので，クライアントとの協力関係を築くことに気を配る」と，ギョー・オバタは説明する．「私たちにとって最も重要な仕事は，しばしば，プロジェクトに関わる人々の心の中や互いに共有するアイディアの中から起こる」．

会長会は依然として経営の中心であるが，一方で，最近，コミュニケーション，財務，人材育成など設計分野以外の専門家が HOK の中枢スタッフに加えられている．これにより，各地の事務所が全体を反映しつつ，ある程度自律的に機能するのを助ける中枢組織が強化される結果となった．

組織的な指針に優先する相互関係の重視，これは大いに HOK の精神の一部を形成するものだが，HOK の規模拡大によって新たな経営構造が必要になっている現在でも，相変わらず HOK においてはこの考え方が明らかにみられる．最も公式的なところでは，HOK の幹部社員によって構成され，会長会にたいして助言を行う取締役会において顕著に表れている．

創造性に満ちた仕事を奨励する HOK の価値観は，設計，エンジニアリング，プランニング，インテリア，およびマーケティングとプロジェクト管理などの各分野を代表して組織される全国役員会の非公式ネットワークにも表れている．これらの役員会は，制作プロセスに対する組織規模での集中を保証することで，分野内の対話を促進しチーム・アプローチの力を拡大するものである．

HOK の成長とともに，引きつづきプロジェクトの種類の多様化，多分野からのアプローチ，そして最終的によい設計とクライアントの満足に結び付くような思慮深く，クライアント本位のプロセスに力を注いでいる．スタウダー副会長のいう，経営効率は「よい設計を助けるものとして遂行されねばならず，私たちがこの仕事の業績向上に努めるのは，ひとえに，より創造性を高める手段としてのことだ」，という認識が，HOK の精神に深く根づいているのである．

Introduction to Projects

HOK のプロジェクト

Since its inception, HOK has remained committed to working on a wide range of projects and building types. Among the notable achievements of the firm are some of the largest and most complex design and construction projects in the world.

Considering the size of the firm and the scope of its work, HOK's design approach is surprisingly subtle. Derived from Gyo Obata's functional perspective of the architect's work, the HOK stamp on a building is nearly invisible, preferring instead fidelity to client and context.

Obata describes this method as design "from the inside out." Its manifestation is design that seeks to imbed itself thoroughly in strategy and intention.

If there is a common attribute that clearly distinguishes these projects, it may be the thoughtful integration of elements within the whole, and of the whole to the physical and social contexts in which it exists. This wholistic approach often expresses itself in a preference for organic shapes and schemes of organization. In many cases, this results in a central space from which others evolve.

The natural contexts of site and natural lighting patterns also serve as prime determinants in the formulation of design strategy, with special emphasis on the close relationship of interior spaces to the availability of sunlight, exterior views, and surrounding architecture. Much thought is given as well to the careful selection of materials chosen for their appropriateness, as well as texture and color. Since many of the firm's projects could easily dominate their surroundings, their visual impression is carefully controlled to be appropriate to the circumstances.

One way of seeing the HOK approach to design is to notice its careful presentation and the way it often serves as a reflection of its environment. This quality of deference is a hallmark of HOK projects, whether they be high-rise, urban office towers, surburban multi-use complexes, or extensive corporate campuses. Careful inspection will reveal a strong and balanced relationship not only between the individual elements of a project, but between the project and its surroundings as well.

"Only after I completely understand all the variables," explains Gyo Obata, "does finding a design for the project become a factor. First, I must understand what purpose that design will fulfill."

"My approach has been influenced by the dominant traditions of the 20th century, mainly the functionalism of the great Modernist architects. But I also am concerned with the variations that give a design life and make it a positive force in peoples' lives."

"What I hope is demonstrated in the whole of these projects is my great respect for the traditions of architecture and my attempt to put them to use, along with the considerable resources of HOK, on behalf of an integrated design approach that meets real goals and serves a real purpose."

HOK はその設立当初から幅広いプロジェクト，多様な建築に携わりつづけている．この設計事務所のおもな業績の中には，世界的にも最大規模あるいは最も複雑なデザインや構造のプロジェクトが含まれている．

この設計事務所の規模とその仕事の範囲を考えると，HOK の設計方法は，非常にとらえがたい．ギョー・オバタの機能本位の建築思想に派生して，建物に現れるHOK の個性はほとんど目に見えない．その代わりクライアントや状況に忠実なものとなっている．

オバタはこの方法を「内から外への」設計という．「設計そのものを，戦略と意図の中に完全に埋没させようとする設計としてそれは現れる」．

これらのプロジェクトをはっきりと特徴づける共通の特性があるとすれば，それは全体の中での個々の要素を統合する配慮，そしてさらに，全体そのものが存在する物理的社会的状況に全体を統合させる思慮深さであるかもしれない．

この方法は，しばしば有機的な形態や構成をとって表現される．多くの場合，これは，そこから種々のスペースが展開する基点となる中心空間を生むことになる．

設計方針を定めるにあたっては，敷地の自然環境や自然光の具合も根本的な決定要因であり，特に日射や外部の景観や周囲の建物の利用と内部空間との密接な関係が重視される．また，適切な資材，質感，色合いの慎重な選択にも多くの考慮がなされる．HOK のプロジェクトは，容易に周囲をその影響下においてしまうものが多いため，それらの視覚的な印象が周囲の環境にふさわしいものであるように注意深くコントロールされる．

HOK の設計思想を理解する一つの方法は，その慎重な表現と，それがしばしば周囲の環境の反映として機能している方法に気づくことである．この謙虚な特性が，都市の高層オフィス・ビル，郊外の多目的ビル，あるいは広大な敷地に建つ企業の施設，それらの如何を問わず，HOK のプロジェクトに共通する特徴である．注意深くみると，プロジェクトの個々の要素間のみならず，プロジェクトとその周辺環境との間にも，強く均斉のとれた関係が発見できるだろう．

「あらゆる変数を完全に理解してはじめて，そのプロジェクトのための設計を考えるという段階になる．まず，その設計が満たすべき目的を理解しなければならない」．

「私の方法は，20世紀の主流の伝統，主として偉大なモダニズムの建築家たちの機能主義の影響を受けてきた．しかし，私はまた，設計に活力を与え，設計を人々の生活の中の実際的な力にする様々な変化にも関心をもっている」．

「私がこれらのプロジェクト全体に表現されてほしいと願うものは，建築の伝統にたいする私の大いなる敬意と，HOK の優秀なスタッフとともに，真の目標を満たし真の目的にかなう統合的な設計方法のために，その伝統を用いる私の意図である」．

Priory Chapel

St. Louis, Missouri, USA

プライアリー・チャペル
アメリカ，ミズーリ州セントルイス
1962

The Priory Chapel grew from the desire of a group of Benedictine monks, newly arrived in the United States from Great Britain, for a contemporary interpretation of their Roman Catholic faith. Choosing the site's highest elevation for the building, the Benedictines asked only that seating for both the monastic choir and lay worshippers be located close to the chapel's main altar, and that twelve side altars be provided for individual worship.

These considerations led naturally to a circular arrangement, in which the scheme of repeated arches fit perfectly. The arches conform to precise parabolic equations, imparting a sense of order to the building. The lower ring of 20 arches contains the entrances, the organ and the side altars. The middle tier provides clerestory lighting and marks the nave of the chapel, while the upper arches form a strongly articulated bell tower.

A five-ton block of granite, illuminated by a roseate skylight, constitutes the main altar and central focus of the chapel's 25,500-square-foot interior. Pews, holding as many as 1,000 worshippers, radiate from the altar in concentric circles, split by evenly spaced aisles.

The individual arches are glazed with a double-sheeted, insulating fiberglass. The exterior sheets are charcoal gray and the interior sheets are white. This arrangement provides a soft, glowing light to the interior during the day and diffuses the interior lighting at night, reversing the visual impression both inside and out. Natural oak furnishings, which rest on a brick-like ceramic tile floor, complete the interior.

グレート・ブリテンから新しくアメリカにやってきたベネディクト会修道士たち．プライアリー・チャペルは，ローマ・カトリックにたいする彼らの信仰を現代的に表現したいという希望から生まれた．ベネディクト僧たちは，まず敷地の中で最も高い場所を選び，そして彼らの出した条件は聖歌隊席と信徒の座席の位置をチャペルの主聖壇の近くにすることと，12の小さな聖壇を個々の礼拝のためにつくるということだけであった．

これらを考慮した結果，自然に導き出されたものは，連続アーチが完璧に調和する環状の配置であった．アーチは正確に放物線を描き，建物にある種の秩序を付加している．20のアーチから成る下部の輪形には，入口，オルガン，小さな聖壇が含まれ，中間部の環は高窓をもちチャペルの身廊の輪郭を暗示しており，上部のアーチによって鐘楼は，強調された形態となっている．

5トンの花崗岩でつくられた主聖壇は，ばら色の天光で照らされ，2万5,500平方フィートのチャペル内部の中心となっている．1,000人の礼拝者を収容できる信徒席は等間隔に通路で分割され，同心円を成して放射線状に広がる．

ひとつひとつのアーチには二重の防音ファイバー・グラスがはめ込まれており，外側のガラスはチャコール・グレーで内側のガラスは白である．この組合せは，日中は内部に柔らかに輝く光をもたらし，夜間は内部の照明を散光させ，内と外の両方で視覚的な印象を逆転させる．天然オークの調度品が煉瓦状の陶器タイルの床に置かれ，インテリアを引き締めている．

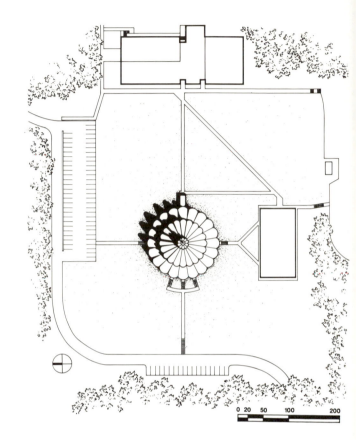

0 20 50 100 200

(above) Site plan.
(below) Floor plan.
(p.23) Benedictine monks framed by a window arch.
(pp.24-25) View from the southwest.
Photo *(p.23)* by Burt Glinn.
Photo *(pp.24-25)* by George Cott.
Photos *(pp.26-27)* by Robert Pettus.

（上）配置図．
（下）平面図．
(p.23) アーチの前で祈りを捧げるベネディクト会修道士たち．
(p.24-25) 南西側から見た外観．

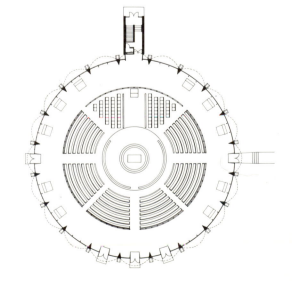

(above) Detail showing a granite side altar in front of fiberglass-glazed window arches.
(p.27) View of the chapel's interior, showing natural oak seating, brick-like ceramic flooring, and the skylight over the granite altar block.

（上）ファイバーグラスをはめ込んだアーチの前に置かれた小さな大理石の聖壇を見る.
（p.27）チャペル内部を見る.天然オークの椅子,煉瓦状の陶器タイルの床,大理石の聖壇の上のスカイライトが見える.

Carrier Chapel

Mississippi University for Women, Columbus, Mississippi, USA

ミシシッピ女子大学キャリア・チャペル
アメリカ，ミシシッピ州コロンバス
1963

Designed to serve as a non-sectarian retreat from the pressures of university life, the Carrier Chapel's symmetrical design, simple materials and natural lighting combine to create a sense of serenity within its walls.

Sited on a low earthen platform, in the center of a small wooded area bounded by other university buildings, the chapel's angular exterior is faced in a dark, reddish-brown brick. The roof and slab are of poured concrete, shaped by random rough board forms to provide a varied texture. A free-standing belltower further emphasizes the linear details of the one-story structure.

The chapel includes just three spaces: a sanctuary that holds up to 150 people; a small niche that forms the chancel; and a vestibule, located between brick piers on the east side of the building, which contains stairs leading up to the sanctuary and down to the basement. The chancel receives direct sunlight from the side and from a small skylight above, making it the focus of attention. The basic configuration of the chapel is a cross on a square, with the walls of the sanctuary forming the square and piers of brick supporting the concrete beams that bear the weight of the roof slab forming the arms of the cross. A narrow strip of glass, placed between the top of the wall and the coffered ceiling, admits a soft, natural light and visually opens up the sanctuary space. It also gives the roof the appearance of floating above the chapel's walls. Lattice-like openwork areas in the interior walls and a two-inch gap between the bottom of the walls and floor add to the building's sense of lightness and grace.

キャリア・チャペルは，大学生活のプレッシャーを遁れる無宗派の黙想の場として設計され，その対称性，シンプルな材質，自然光が調和して，壁の内側に静穏な場を生み出している．

チャペルは大学の諸施設に囲まれた小さな森の中央にある低い台地にあって，その正方形の外観には，濃い赤茶色の煉瓦が貼られている．屋根と天井スラブはラフボード・コンクリート打ち放しで，変化に富んだ肌合いを出している．独立した鐘楼は，この平家建築の直線的なディテールをさらに強調している．チャペルの内部は三つの空間に分かれるのみである．すなわち，150人まで収容できる聖堂，内陣になっている小さな壁龕，そして建物の東側の煉瓦の柱に挟まれた，階段室のある入口ホールである．内陣には側面と小さな天窓からの直射日光が入り，注意を引くようになっている．チャペルの基本的な構成は，方形の広場のうえの十字架を表現しており，聖堂の壁が方形の広場を表わし，屋根のスラブの重量がかかるコンクリートの梁を支える煉瓦の支柱が十字架の腕を表す．壁の上端と格天井との間にはめこまれた細いガラスの帯からは，柔らかな自然光が射し込み，聖堂を広く見せる．また，屋根がチャペルの壁の上に浮かんでいるような感じを与えている．内壁の格子様の透かし細工の部分および壁の下端と床の間の2インチの段差が，建物に軽さと優雅さを加えている．

(*above*) Site plan.
(*p.29*) *Interior view of the chapel, looking toward the chancel.*
(*pp.30-31*) *Carrier Chapel, showing main entrance with fountain in the foreground.*
Photos (pp.28-31) by Bud Hunter.

(上) 配置図.
(p.29) チャペル内部，内陣の方を見る.
(p.30-31) チャペルのメイン・エントランスの方から見る.手前に泉が見える.

National Air and Space Museum

The Smithsonian Institution, Washington, D.C., USA

国立航空宇宙博物館
アメリカ，ワシントン D.C.，スミソニアン博物館
1976

The National Air and Space Museum occupies a prestigious location on the Capitol Mall, the site of several historic structures including the U.S. Capitol Building. Commissioned to commemorate the nation's remarkable achievements in flight, the Museum's location required that it be a fitting complement to its important neighbors, especially the National Gallery of Art, which it faces.

Opened July 1, 1976, and described by former President Gerald Ford as the United States' "birthday gift to itself," the National Air and Space Museum is generally regarded as the most-visited museum in the world, hosting approximately 10 million visitors per year. The primary function of the Museum is the display of a substantial collection of enormous machinery (approximately 65 aircraft and 100 spacecraft).

The museum is formed from simple design elements: four geometric blocks, clad in a marble that matches the exterior of the National Gallery, alternate with three glass-enclosed exhibit bays. These glass bays supply the dominant visual focus, creating what *Newsweek* magazine described as "an outdoor spaciousness and freedom totally unexpected in a building so packed with displays."

The circulation system is a key element of the museum's design, and has allowed it to accommodate much larger crowds than were originally anticipated. The main circulation path on both levels parallels the course of the Capitol Mall, making it easy for visitors to orient themselves as they go through the various exhibit halls. The 630,000-square-foot structure also contains a research library, administrative offices, and two theaters: a 485-seat auditorium with curved 55-foot by 75-foot screen designed for IMAX curved-projection, and the Albert Einstein Spacearium, a 245-seat domed planetarium designed for simulated flight and space presentations. In 1988, HOK designed a glass-enclosed, 1,000-seat restaurant which connects to the east end of the Museum. The facility actually contains two restaurants: the Flight Line, a cafeteria-style restaurant, and The Wright Place, a table service restaurant. Both provide museum visitors with spectacular views of the Capitol Building and the Mall, as well as fine food.

(*right*) *Site plan.*
(*p.33*) *Detail of restaurant and museum.*
(*pp.34–35*) *View from the capitol Mall.*
Photo (*p.33*) *by George Silk.*
Photos (*pp.34–39*) *by George Cott.*

(右) 配置図.
(p.33) レストランと博物館外観詳細.
(p.34-35) 議事堂モールより見る.

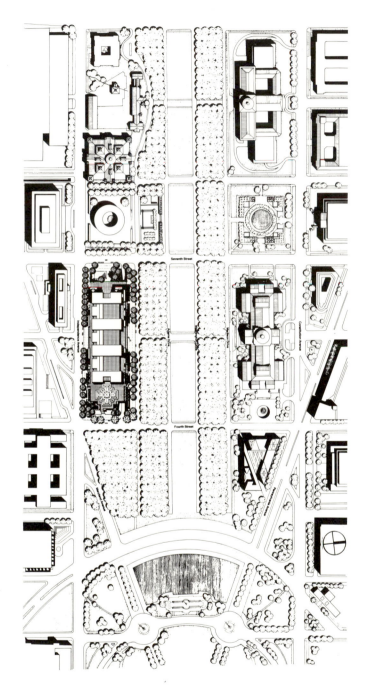

国立航空宇宙博物館は，合衆国議事堂などの歴史的建築がある議事堂モールの格式ある場所にある．アメリカ航空史の優れた業績を記念するという使命を担うこの博物館は，位置的に，周囲の重要な建物，特に真向いにある国立美術館と調和する必要があった．

1976年7月1日にオープンし，ジェラルド・フォード元大統領がアメリカ合衆国の「自分自身へのバースデイ・プレゼント」と呼んだ国立航空宇宙博物館は，年間約1,000万人の入館者を誇り，世界で最も人気のある博物館として広く認められている．この博物館の第一の機能は巨大な機械類（飛行機約65機，宇宙船約100機）の充実したコレクションの展示である．

この博物館はシンプルな設計要素によって構成されている．国立美術館の外観に調和する大理石でできた四つの幾何学的形態をしたブロックがあり，ガラスで囲まれた三つの展示室と交互になっている．このガラス張りの部屋は優れた視覚的なポイントとして，『ニューズウィーク』が「展示物が密集した建物の中とは思えないほどまったく意外な戸外のような広さと自由さ」と表現した雰囲気をつくり出している．

動線システムは設計上の重要な要素の一つであり，当初予想したよりもずっと多くの人数に対応することができるようになった．中心となる展示動線は上下階とも議事堂モールに平行しており，見学者が様々な展示ホールを通り抜ける際に自分自身の位置を把握しやすくなっている．

この63万平方フィートの博物館には，研究用図書室，本部オフィス，および二つの劇場も備えられている．劇場の一つは485席のIMAX曲面映写用の55×75フィートの曲面スクリーンの劇場で，もう一つは飛行状態や宇宙空間のシュミレーション用に設計された245席のドーム型プラネタリウムである，アルバート・アインシュタイン・スペサリウムである．

1988年，HOKは博物館の東端につづく1,000席のガラス張りのレストランを設計した．これは現実には二つのレストランから成る．一つはカフェテリア方式の「フライト・ライン」，もう一つはテーブル方式の「ライト・プレイス」である．ともに，訪れる人々においしい食事だけではなく国会議事堂やモールの壮観な展望をも提供する．

(right top to bottom)   (右上から下へ)
Third-level plan.   3階平面図．
First-level plan.   1階平面図．
Cross section.   横断面図．
Longitudinal section.   長手方向断面図．
(p.37) Visitors entering the   (p.37) 展示室「飛行への道標」．立体トラ
"Milestones of Flight"   スを見る．
gallery.   (p.38-39) 航空運輸展示室．
(pp.38-39) The Air
Transportation Gallery.

Legend
1-Library
2-Spacearium
3-Offices
4-Cooling tower
5-Dining room
6-Kitchen

0 10 20 50   100

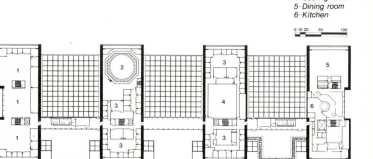

Legend
1-Gallery
2-Museum shop

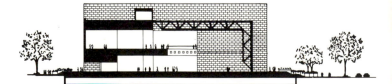

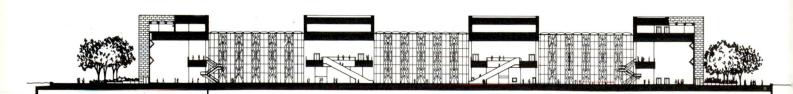

King Saud University

with Gollins Melvin Ward Partnership of London (Joint Venture)
Riyadh, Saudi Arabia

キング・サウド大学
サウジアラビア，リヤド
1984

The program for King Saud University called for a campus for 20,000 students which would combine contemporary efficiency with maximum flexibility for future expansion.

The $4 billion campus is located on a 2,400-acre site on the Najd plateau, 20 miles northwest of the capital city of Riyadh. Complementing its desert setting, the University is designed in a style derived from traditional Najd architecture, with closely set buildings, shaded walkways and small, deep-seated window openings that shelter building users from the harsh desert sun while creating an interesting interplay of light and shadow. These elements have been restated in a modular, precast building system, allowing maximum efficiency in construction.

A tree-lined roadway that leads to the University Plaza provides a formal entrance to the University. Across from the arrival plaza is a large mosque, which is located adjacent to the Forum, the heart of the campus. This vast skylit space is formed by the library, theater, University Center and administration buildings, and serves as the focal point for university life.

Radiating out from the Forum, three covered walkways or "spines" lead to each of the university's divisions: science, medicine, and the arts. These divisions contain, collectively, ten colleges, each of which is identified by a different design motif and marked along the walkways by a skylighted plaza. Located beneath the main spine, a utility tunnel connects to the below-grade level of each three-level academic building. Students enter the colleges on the second level, which is slightly above grade, and, thus, never have to go up or down more than one flight of stairs to reach their classrooms.

Significant in the design of King Saud University are 45 gardens and courtyards, some quite elaborate. In the Forum, fountains supplement the rich vocabulary of materials and landscaping. Construction of the university—which required 6,000 working drawings, 10,000 sheets of specifications, two precast factories built in the desert, and almost 11,000 employees during construction—was accomplished in 40 months. HOK provided the master plan for the University and was the lead firm in a consortium called HOK+4 that supervised design and construction. The project plan also provides for expansion to double the present student population.

(above right) Site plan.
(p.41) *Pedestrian spine with*
library in the background.
Photos (pp.40-47) by
Robert Azzi.

（右上）配置図.
（p.41）歩道を見る．奥に見えるのは図
書館.

Legend
1-College of agriculture
2-College of engineering
3-College of science
4-College of administrative science
5-College of education
6-College of arts
7-College of pharmacy
8-College of dentistry
9-College of medicine
10-Mosque platform
11-Library
12-Formal entrance
13-Auditoria building
14-Forum
15-Student housing
16-Staff housing

キング・サウド大学の計画は，時代に合った効率性と将来の拡張にも最大限に対応しうる能力を兼ね備えた，2万人の学生のためのキャンパスを必要とするものであった.

40億ドルのキャンパスは，首都リヤドの北西20マイルにあるネジド高原の2,400エーカーの土地にある. 砂漠という環境を補うため，この大学は，伝統的なネジド建築に基づいて設計されている. たとえば，建物を密集させたり，日除けのある歩道を設けたり，あるいはまた，光と影の交錯する面白さを生かしながら利用者を厳しい砂漠の日射から守るみぎりの深い小さな窓をつけたりしている. これらの要素は，建設の際の効率をはかるため，基準寸法のプレキャスト・システムで行われた.

街路樹の連なる広場に至る道が大学の玄関口となっている. 広場の入口の向かい側には大きなモスクがあり，その隣にはキャンパスの中心であるフォーラムがある. この広大な自然光の射し込む空間は図書館，劇場，大学センター，本部ビル群によって構成されており，大学生活の中枢地点となっている.

フォーラムからは，3本の屋根付きの歩道が放射状に「背骨」のように，科学，医学，芸術の各領域に伸びている. これらには総計10のカレッジがあり，各カレッジは異なったデザイン・モチーフで区別され，歩道沿いにスカイライトのある広場によって明示されている. この背骨の下にある通路は3階建ての教室棟のそれぞれの地下階に通じている. 学生は地上レヴェルより少し高い2階からカレッジに入るので，教室にゆくためには上または下に1回だけ階段を上り下りすればすむ.

キング・サウド大学の設計において重要なのは，45の庭および中庭で，そのうちいくつかは非常に手が込んでいる. フォーラムにおいては，種々の材料や情趣豊かな表現に噴水が加わり，みごとなものになっている.

建設には6,000枚の作業用設計図，1万枚の仕様書，砂漠に建てられた二つのプレキャスト工場，それに1万1,000人に近い人員を要し，40ヵ月で完成をみた. HOKは，大学側にマスター・プランを提供し，設計および建設を監督したHOK＋4と呼ばれた共同企業体の中枢であった. このプロジェクト計画はまた現在の学生数が2倍になった際の増築をも見越したものである.

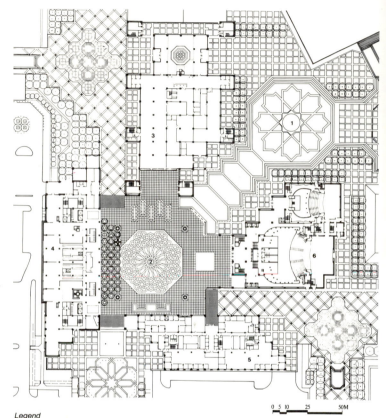

Legend
1-Formal entrance
2-Forum
3-Library
4-University center
5-Administration building
6-Auditoria building

(pp.42-43) Overall view of the campus in early evening.
(above right) A part of the second floor plan.
(below) East-west section through the Forum.
(p.45) College building viewed from covered walkway.

(p.42-43) 夕暮れ時のキャンパス全景.
(右上) フォーラム周辺部の2階平面図.
(下) フォーラムを通る東西方向断面図.
(p.45) 屋根付きの歩道から大学の建物群を見る.

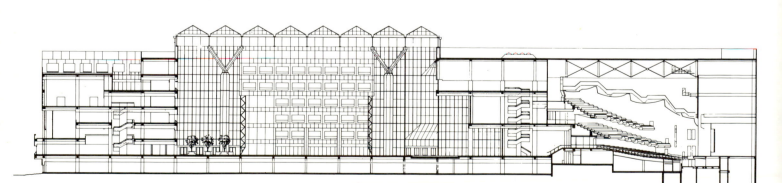

(top) Detail of steel truss system and concrete column supporting the skylight roof over the Forum.
(above) The elaborate marble floor pattern of the Forum.
(p.47) View across the Forum to the library entrance.

（上）フォーラムにかかるスカイライト・ルーフを支えるコンクリート柱とスティールのトラス構造.
（下）精巧な大理石パターンによるフォーラムの床.
（p.47）フォーラム．図書館入口を正面に見る.

George R. Moscone Convention Center

with Jack Young & Associates
San Francisco, California, USA

ジョージ・R・モスコーン・コンヴェンション・センター
アメリカ, カリフォルニア州サンフランシスコ

1981

Built mostly underground to satisfy the city's active "no growth" movement, the 650,000-square-foot Moscone Convention Center brought major convention bookings back to San Francisco and spurred new development in the area south of Market Street. The center's 275,000-square-foot main exhibit hall is supported by eight pairs of post-tensioned concrete arches anchored to massive concrete foundation beams. The arch frame design provides for a totally column-free exhibit space, creating an open and airy feeling in this underground space. The clear span also increases the hall's flexibility. The facility also includes a 30,000-square-foot ballroom with a 25-foot clear ceiling height which can hold up to 4,000 people.

A 42,000-square-foot lobby, the only portion of the facility that is located above-ground, links all the convention center's public spaces. The lobby has glass walls and a roof supported by five-foot-deep steel girders spanning four single-piece steel trusses, each of which is 120 feet long and 90 feet on center. The trusses are anchored on one end at the cantilevered arch abutments and on the other by X-bracing on the huge, post-tensioned tunnel exits. The roof slides on the truss work to allow for normal expansion and contraction due to temperature changes, and are designed to handle the seismic loading that would occur during an earthquake.

A mezzanine level, located ten feet below the lobby entrance, contains 34 meeting rooms and the center's administrative offices.

同市の活発な「ノー・グロウス（無成長）」運動に合せて大半が地下に建設された65万平方フィートのモスコーン・コンヴェンション・センターは，大きな会議の開催をサンフランシスコに呼び戻し，また，マーケット・ストリート南側の新しい開発に拍車をかける役割も果たした．

このセンターの27万5,000平方フィートの主展示ホールは，巨大なコンクリートの基礎梁に固定された8組のポストテンション・コンクリートのアーチで支えられている．このアーチによって無柱の展示空間となり，この地下空間を広々として落ちついた雰囲気にしている．また，この長スパンによりホールのフレキシビリティが一層高められている．センター内には，4,000人まで収容可能な25フィートもの高い天井をもつ3万平方フィートのバンケット・ホールが備えられている．

施設のうち唯一地上にある4万2,000平方フィートのロビーは，コンヴェンション・センターのすべての公共スペースに通じている．ロビーにはガラス壁があり，屋根は梁成5フィートのスティール製大梁で支えられ，長さ120フィート，心々で，90フィートのスティール・トラス四つをつないでいる．トラスは一方の端をキャンティレヴァーのアーチ台に固定され，他方の端はX形の支柱によって巨大なポスト・テンション方式の坑道出口に固定されている．屋根は，温度変化による通常の伸縮に対応するためトラスの上をスライドし，また地震の際の荷重に対応できるよう設計されている．

中2階は，ロビー入口より10フィート下にあって34の会議室とこのセンターの管理事務室がある．

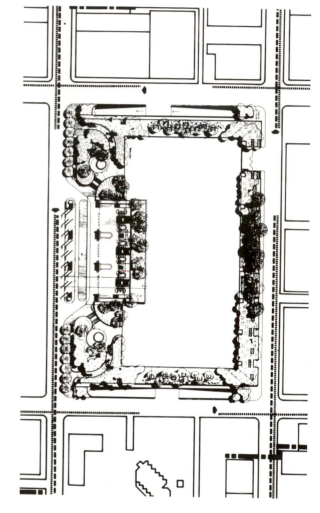

(above) Site plan.
(below) Cross section.
(p.49) Overall view of Moscone Center, looking west, with the San Francisco skyline in the background.
(pp.50-51) Angled view of entrance at twilight, showing the X-bracing of the steel truses that support the roof. Photos (pp.48-57) by Peter Aaron／Esto.

（上）配置図．
（下）横断面図．
(p.49) 東側からの遠景．背後にサンフランシスコの町並みが見える．
(p.50-51) 入口部分．屋根を支えるスティール・トラスのX形の支柱が見える．

Legend
1-Lobby
2-Mechanical
3-Ballroom
4-Exhibit hall

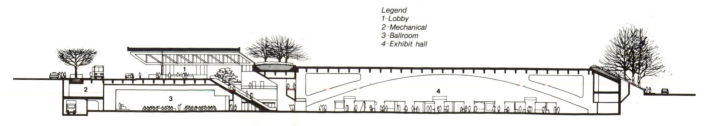

(p.52) Supporting truss and glass curtainwall detail, from inside the lobby.
(above) Looking east across stairs and seating modules.
(pp.54-55) Arch-framing in main exhibit hall.

(p.52) ロビーの中から支柱とガラス壁を見る.
(上) 屋内で東側を見る. 階段と談話コーナーが見える.
(p.54-55) 主展示ホールのアーチ.

(*above*) *Boat show in the main exhibit hall, viewed through the arch framing.* (*p.57*) *Arch-frame and mezzanine-level suite viewed from center of exhibit hall.*

（上）主展示ホールでのボート・ショーをアーチ越しに見る.
（p.57）展示ホールのアーチ・フレームとその間の会議室を見る.

Dallas Galleria

with Kendall/Heaton/Associates
Dallas, Texas, USA

ダラス・ガレリア
アメリカ，テキサス州ダラス
1983

With obvious reference to historic urban meeting places, such as the Galleria in Milan and Rockefeller Center in New York City, the Galleria in Dallas has become a major urban focus. Occupying a 44-acre site, the multi-use complex includes a shopping mall, two major retail outlets, commercial office space, a luxury hotel, an athletic club, and parking for 12,000 cars.

At the heart of the Galleria is a three-level, 1,200-foot-long shopping mall covered by a vaulted skylight. Boldly articulated trusswork supports the energy-efficient skylight glass, allowing as much sunlight as possible to enter the complex. The mall widens at its center to create an atrium court which encloses a large skating rink. The design of the Galleria is unified by the consistent use of materials, particularly polished and reflective surfaces. Two textures of precast rose-colored, granite-aggregate concrete are used throughout.

Complementing the soft tone of the concrete are solar panels of gray glass, silver metallic paneling, and accents of polished granite, mirror-finish stainless steel, and granite paving.

A further unifying effect is created by the use of circular and vaulted forms in conjunction with rectangles to create highly identifiable silhouettes. This can be seen clearly in the office towers and in the hotel, the most visible element against the skyline. The design of the hotel's glass entry canopy repeats the triple-tiered cascading vaults of its top.

ミラノのガレリアやニューヨークのロックフェラー・センターなどの歴史的な都市の広場を参照して，ダラスのガレリアは都市の大きな中心となった．44エーカーもの敷地を占有するこの多目的コンプレックス（複合ビル）には，ショッピング・モール，二つの大型店舗，オフィス・スペース，高級ホテル，アスレチック・クラブ，1万2,000台収容可能な駐車場などがある．

ガレリアの中心は，アーチ形のスカイ・ライトで覆われた長さ1,200フィートの3層吹抜けになったショッピング・モールである．大胆なデザインのトラスがエネルギー効率のよいスカイ・ライトのガラスを支え，コンプレックスの中に日光を最大限に採り入れている．モールは中央部で幅が広くなっており，大きなスケート・リンクを囲む広場になっている．

ガレリアの設計には，素材へのこだわり，特に研磨仕上げと反射面をもつ素材を一貫して使用することによって統一感が出されており，ばら色の，そして花崗岩粒の入った2種の肌合いのプレキャスト・コンクリートが全体を通して使用されている．グレーのガラスのソーラー・パネルやシルヴァー・メタルのパネルに加えて，研磨仕上げの花崗岩と鏡のようなステンレス・スティール，花崗岩の敷石のアクセントなどが，コンクリートの柔らかなトーンを補完している．

きわめて識別しやすい矩形と合せて，円形あるいはアーチ形を使うことによってさらに統一的効果がつくり出されている．このことはスカイラインを背景に最大の視覚的要素となるオフィス・タワーやホテルにおいて顕著に見られる．ホテル入口のガラスでつくられた天蓋のデザインは，ホテルの頂部が3層のヴォールトの段状の連なりとなっているのを反映している．

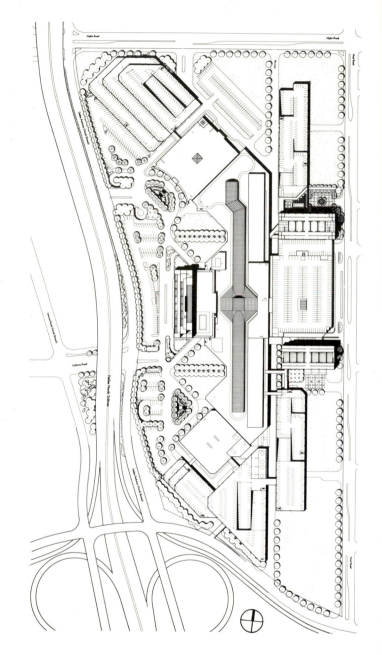

(*above*) Site plan.
(*p.59*) Two Galleria Tower in foreground and One Galleria Tower in rear at left.
(*pp.60-61*) View of Dallas Galleria mixed-use complex from the southwest.
Photos (*p.58-65*) by George Cott.

（上）配置図
(p.59) 手前に第2ガレリア・タワーを，その後ろ左手に第1ガレリア・タワーを見る．
(p.60-61) 南西からダラス・ガレリア複合ビルを見る．

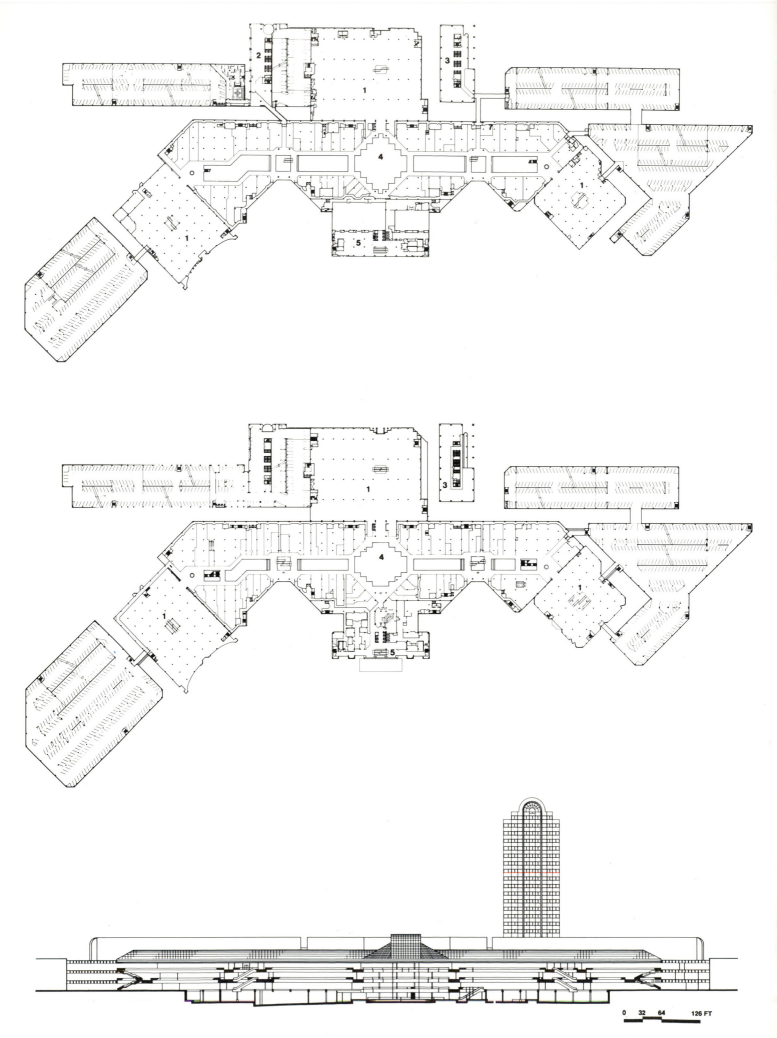

0   32   64   126 FT

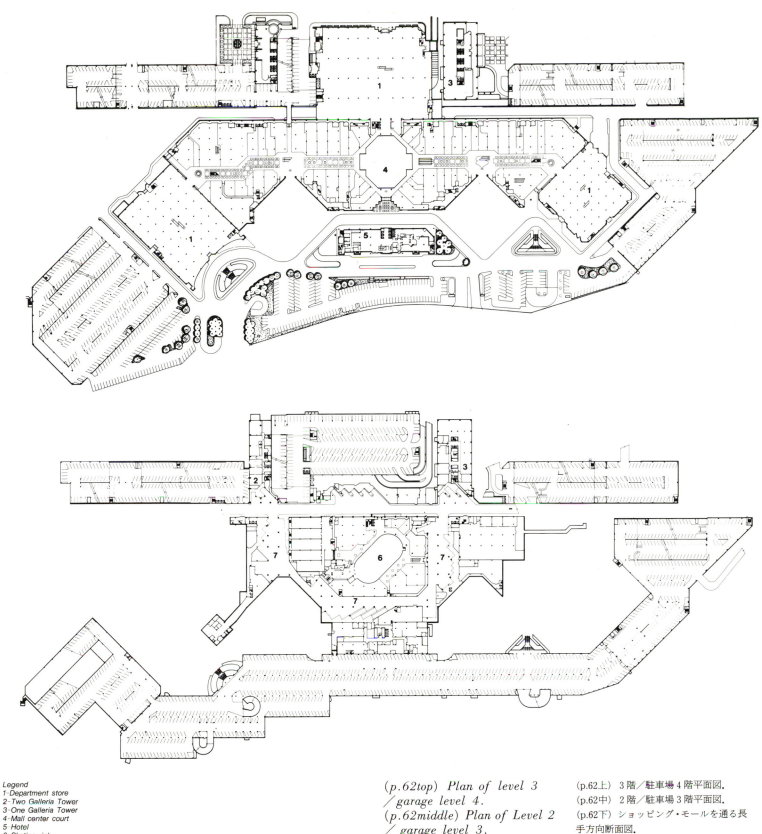

Legend
1-Department store
2-Two Galleria Tower
3-One Galleria Tower
4-Mall center court
5-Hotel
6-Skating rink
7-Truck concourse

(p.62top) *Plan of level 3 / garage level 4.*
(p.62middle) *Plan of Level 2 / garage level 3.*
(p.62bottom) *Longitudinal section through shopping mall.*
(top) *Plan of level 1 / garage level 1.*
(above) *Plan of rink level / garage level B1.*

（p.62上）3階／駐車場4階平面図.
（p.62中）2階／駐車場3階平面図.
（p.62下）ショッピング・モールを通る長手方向断面図.
（上）1階／駐車場1階平面図.
（下）スケート・リンク階／駐車場地下1階平面図.

(*above*) *Terrace above skating rink at center court.* (*p.65*) *The Galleria's retail mall* (*center*) *extends from the center court.*

（上）センター・コートのスケート・リンクの上に張り出したテラス．
（p.65）センター・コートからガレリアのショッピング・モール（中央部分）を見る．

King Khalid International Airport

Riyadh, Saudi Arabia

キング・ハリド国際空港
サウジアラビア，リヤド
1983

In a desert setting 22 miles north of Riyadh, Saudi Arabia, the complex design of King Khalid International Airport interprets elements of the Islamic architectural tradition in forms which signal the era of jet flight. Selected for the country's leaders by the Bechtel Corporation, HOK provided services ranging from site planning to interior design, and from the selection of patterned tile for the many mosaics to the design of the royal silverware.

Set above parking for 11,000 cars, the airport is intended to accommodate 15 million visitors by the turn of the century, serving as a practical and symbolic gateway to both the country and culture of Saudi Arabia.

At the center of the airport is the country's largest mosque. Hexagonal in plan and 170 feet long on each side, its massive domed roof seems to float on triangulated clerestory arches. Extending from the mosque are garden walkways to five terminals—two domestic and two international, and a private royal terminal.

Each terminal is organized as a large open pavilion surrounding an oasis-like garden-court and covered by a gently curved roof of interlocking triangles suspended over clerestory arches. Arriving passengers pass through the garden court on their way to the immigration office, and departing passengers view the garden-court from avove as they go to the airport's waiting areas prior to leaving the country.

The royal terminal includes a reception hall, a 100-seat auditorium, offices, guest suites, and the King's quarters. Plazas, landscaped roadways, and mechanized sidewalks link the complex of buildings. Several of the airport's organizing themes were derived from Islamic religious and secular structures. The most prominent is the use of triangular relationships, especially of 30 and 60 degrees, as a unifying element. Other elements drawn from traditional Islamic architecture are the use of profuse geometric motifs, gracefully filtered sunlight, and the generous arrangement of gardens, arcades and fountains.

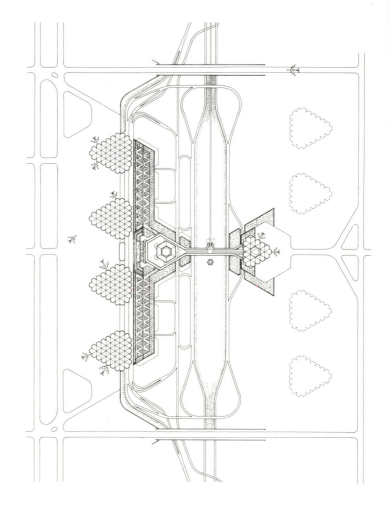

この計画はリヤドの北方22マイルの砂漠中に，イスラム建築の伝統的要素をジェット機時代の到来を示す形で表現している．HOKは，配置計画からインテリア，モザイクの模様タイル選択から王室用銀器のデザインまで行った．

上層に1万1,000台収容の駐車場を備え，サウジアラビア，およびその文化への入口として，今世紀中に1,500万人の利用を見込んでいる．中心には国内最大のモスクがある．一辺170フィートの六角形で，その巨大なドーム型の屋根は三角形の高窓のアーチの上に浮かんでいるように見える．モスクから歩道が五つのターミナルに伸びているが，二つは国内線，二つは国際線，そして王室専用ターミナルである．各ターミナルは，オアシスのような中庭を囲む大きなパヴィリオンのように配置され，高窓のアーチにつるされた三角形をつないでいる勾配のゆるやかな屋根で覆われている．

王室ターミナルには，レセプション・ホールと100席の講堂，事務室，ゲスト・ルーム，国王の宿舎などがある．

空港を構成するうえでのテーマのいくつかは，イスラムの宗教建築および世俗建築に由来する．最も顕著なのは，統一要素として三角形，特に30度と60度のものの連結を用いたことである．伝統的イスラム建築に由来する他の要素としては，幾何学的モティーフを多用したこと，やさしく射し込む日光，そして庭にアーケードと噴水の組合せを多用したことがあげられる．

(*above*) *Site plan.*
(*p.67*) *Aerial view of King Khalid International Airport. Photos (pp.67, 69) by Robert Azzi. Photos (pp.70-71) by Gregory Murphey.*

（上）配置図．
(p.67) キング・ハリド国際空港遠景．

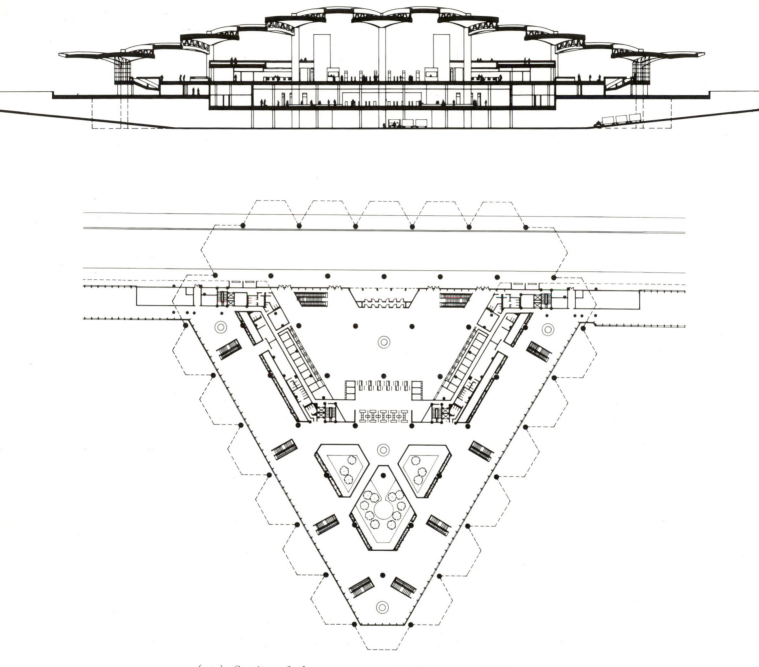

(top) Section of the
passenger terminal.
(above) Departure-level plan.
(p.69) View across a
typical waiting area in a
passenger terminal.

（上）旅客ターミナル断面図.
（下）搭乗階平面図.
（p.69）旅客ターミナルの待合コーナーを
見る.

(*above*) *Intricate tile patterns in the Royal terminal*.
(*p.71*) *View under the dome in the Mosque*.

（上）王室ターミナルの細かいタイル模様.
（p.71）モスクのドーム部分を見る.

St. Louis Union Station

St. Louis, Missouri, USA

セントルイス・ユニオン駅
アメリカ，ミズーリ州セントルイス
1985

The $135 million renovation and redevelopment of St. Louis Union Station, one of the largest mixed-use rehabilitation projects ever undertaken in the United States, combined new construction with meticulous historic restoration. Located on 35 acres at the edge of the St. Louis central business district, the 825,000-square-foot complex includes a 275,000-square-foot retail mall and a 550-room luxury hotel.

Now listed on the National Historic Register, the station was the largest single-level passenger train terminal in the world when it opened in 1894. By the 1970s, it had fallen into disrepair and disuse, the victim of changing patterns in transportation.

The redevelopment project integrated three distinct components of the station into the design of a new urban marketplace. The station's immense headhouse, including a 230-foot clock tower, was restored to its original beauty. The midway, where passengers once boarded their trains, is now a bustling retail center. And the old train shed—the largest single-span train shed in the world, measuring 606 by 810 feet long and reaching 140 feet at the highest point of each truss—was reroofed and reglazed to span the retail area and the new sections of the hotel.

Restoration work was focused on three areas of the headhouse: the barrel-vaulted grand hall, with its gold leaf, stenciling and stained glass; the atrium rotunda and oak dining room; and the Gothic Corridor. Adjoining the headhouse, and leading south under the east side of the train shed, the design team created an L-shaped commercial "street" lined with shops and restaurants. Under the west side of the train shed is a wing containing additional hotel rooms and meeting rooms. Restaurants and hotel rooms at the south end of the complex overlook a landscaped park with a small lake and beer garden.

1億3,500万ドルをかけたセントルイス・ユニオン駅の修復再開発計画は，全米でこれまで企画された最大の多目的施設の修復計画の一つであるが，それは細心の注意を必要とする歴史的建造物の修復と新しい建築とを組み合せたものであった．セントルイスのビジネス街の中心地区のはずれ35エーカーの敷地内の82万5,000平方フィートの施設には，27万5,000平方フィートのショッピング・モールと550室の高級ホテルがある．

現在，全国史跡目録に載っているこの駅は，1894年のオープン当時は世界最大の平家の旅客駅であったが，1970年代までには，輸送手段の変遷の犠牲となり，修理もされず，そのうち使われなくなってしまった．この再開発計画によって，駅の三つの異なった要素が一つの新しい都市型ショッピング・センターとして統合され，230フィートの時計台をもつ広大な駅舎が復元された．以前乗車場であった中央通路は，今や賑やかなショッピング・センターになった．そして，606×810フィートで，各トラスの最高部が140フィートにもなる列車庫としては世界最大の屋根は，葺き替えられガラスを入れ替えられて，ショッピング・エリアと新しいホテル部分との上に架け渡された．

修復は駅舎の三つの区域に集中して行われた．金箔，ステンシル模様のステンド・グラスが使われた半円筒ヴォールト天井の大ホール，円形アトリウムとオーク材仕上げの食堂，そしてゴシック様式の回廊である．この大屋根の下の東側に，駅舎に隣接して南に向かって伸びるL字形の商店・レストラン街をつくった．また西側には新たなホテル客室と会議室のある棟があり，南端に位置するレストランとホテルからは泉水とビア・ガーデンのある公園が見渡せる．

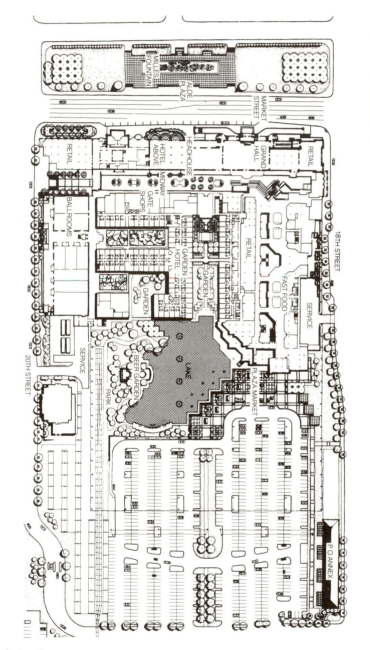

(*above*) *Site plan.*
(*p.73*) *Early morning view of the clock tower and headhouse of St. Louis Union Station.*
Photos (*pp.72-77*) *by Robert Pettus except p.75.*
Photo (*p.75*) *by HOK Photography.*

（上）配置図．
(p.73) 早朝のセントルイス駅の時計塔と駅舎を見る．

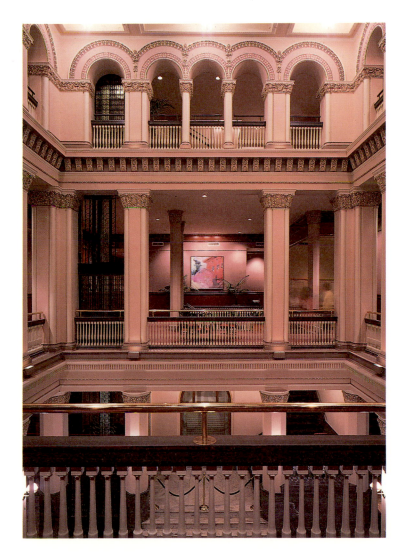

(p.74) *View of the restored barrell-vaulted Grand Hall.* (above) *Lobby area surrounding the restored hotel atrium at Union Station.*

(p.74) 修復された半円筒ヴォールト天井の大ホールを見る.
(上) ユニオン駅のホテルのアトリウムをロビーが回廊のように囲んでいる.

(above) View of hotel complex and restaurants under the train shed, viewed from the south, across the lake.
(p.77) Looking north along the"Retail Street" under the train shed roof. Hotel rooms are visible at left.

（上）泉水越しに南側から見る．列車庫の屋根の下にホテルやレストランが見える．
（p.77）列車庫の屋根の下のショッピング・モールにそって北側を見る．ホテルの部屋が左手に見える．

BP America, Inc., Corporate Headquarters

Cleveland, Ohio, USA

BPアメリカ社本社ビル
アメリカ，オハイオ州クリーヴランド
1986

With the announcement in the early 1980s of plans for a new headquarters in Cleveland, local citizens looked forward to a project that would strengthen the city's economy by uniting 2,500 corporate employees in a prime downtown location. At the same time, however, many worried that a 1.5 million-square-foot building would inevitably dominate the early 20th-century structures around it. Two major historic elements in the area are the Public Square, which contains the Civil War Soldiers and Sailors Monument, and the Terminal Tower, which was constructed in 1930 and has become a symbol of Cleveland's role in the region's industrial growth.

To address these concerns, the tower's height was limited in deference to the Terminal Tower's status as the tallest building in the city. Its eight-story atrium, on a scale with the surrounding buildings, provides an attractive transition from the Public Square to the tower. The atrium faces the square and reflects the monument in its all-glass facade. Inside, retail shops, restaurants and public display areas overlook the lower level of the heavily landscaped atrium, and skywalks to nearby department stores invite the public to enter. Rising behind the atrium, the 45-story tower is marked by a streamlined pattern of vertical setbacks and horizontal facets which give an impression of slimness to the tower's mass. Its central design characteristic is a crease that allows it to parallel significant side streets. The crease also gives the building the impression of unfolding in a gesture of welcome.

The structure is clad in a light-colored Texas red granite, which provides a warm tone that is especially appealing during the city's long, cold winters. Lighting at the corners and top of the tower reinforce the sculptural quality of the building at night.

1980年代初めにクリーヴランドに新本社を建てる計画が発表されると，地元の人々は，これによってダウンタウンの一等地に2,500人の社員が集まり市の経済が活性化されることを期待した．しかし，それと同時に，150万平方フィートのビルが必然的に周囲の20世紀初頭の建築を威圧してしまうことを心配する人も多かった．この地区の二つの主要な歴史的建築物といえば，南北戦争陸海兵の記念碑のある公共広場と，1930年に建てられ，この地域の工業発展にたいするクリーヴランドの役割の象徴となったターミナル・タワーがある．

こうした懸念に対応するため，タワーの高さは市内で最も高い建物としてのターミナル・タワーの地位を脅かさないように抑えられた．周囲の建物と同規模の8層吹抜けのアトリウムは，公共広場とタワーとをつなぐ魅力的なプロムナードになっている．アトリウムは公共広場に面し，ガラスのファサードに，記念碑が反射して映る．内部は，店やレストラン，展示コーナーがあって植樹の施されたアトリウムの下層部分を見渡せるようになっており，また，スカイ・ウォークによって近接するデパートにゆけるようになっている．

アトリウムの背後には，45階建てのタワーがそびえており，垂直方向のセットバックと切子面を構成する長手方向のファサードが建物全体にほっそりしたイメージを与えている．この設計の特徴は，横丁に沿うようにした「く」の字の凹みである．これは，建物に，腕を広げ人々を歓迎しているような印象を与えることにもなっている．

建物表面は明るい色のテキサス産赤花崗岩で覆われ，特にこの町の長くて寒い冬には魅力的で暖かな雰囲気をかもし出している．コーナーおよびタワー頂部の照明によって，夜間は建物の造形美が強調される．

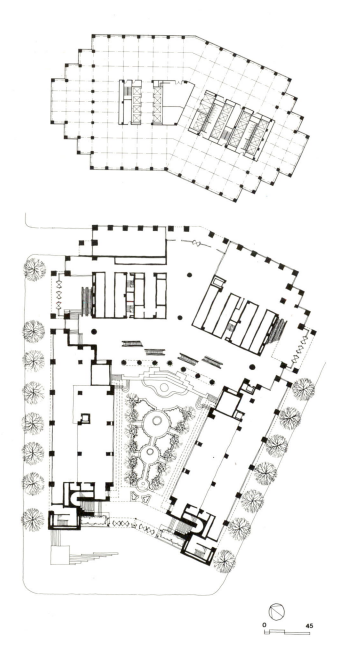

0   45

(*top*) *Typical floor plan.*
(*above*) *First floor plan.*
(*p.79*) *The west facade of the tower, viewed from the Public Square.*
Photos (pp.79-83) by George Cott.

（上）基準階平面図．
（下）1階平面図．
（p.79）タワー西側のファサード．公共広場から見る．

(p.80) *Another view of the tower, from the south, showing its stepped design. (above) Looking west across the atrium at twilight.*

（p.80）タワーを南からみる．段状のセットバックがよくわかる．
（上）黄昏時のアトリウム．

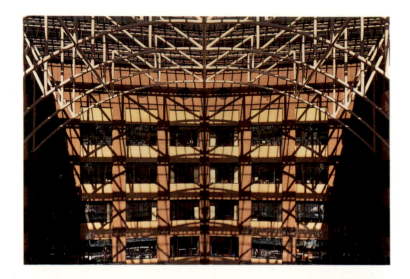

(top) Upper part of the atrium.
(above) Cascade at east end of the atrium.
(p.83) Looking east across the atrium.

(上) アトリウム上部.
(下) アトリウム東端の滝.
(p.83) アトリウム東側を見る.

p2

p3

Kellogg Company Corporate Headquarters

Battle Creek, Michigan, USA

ケロッグ社本社ビル
アメリカ，ミシガン州バトル・クリーク
1986

When the Kellogg Company, a global food products corporation, felt the need to consolidate its operations in a new headquarters, it also wanted to articulate, architecturally, the values that motivate the company's activities. HOK proposed an open, airy headquarters facility to be built on a 17-acre site overlooking a small public park in downtown Battle Creek.

The site was in serious need of renewal, and Kellogg's decision to build there expressed both the company's commitment and gratitude to the citizens of its home city. HOK also served as an active partner with Kellogg and the city of Battle Creek in obtaining a federal grant to landscape a section of the Battle Creek River that runs through the headquarters site.

Since the basic values of America's farming regions contribute significantly to the Kellogg philosophy, its corporate headquarters in every way display a respect for wise stewardship of the land and agrarian culture. This is evident throughout the facility, from the building's low-rise, stepped-back profile to its thematic furnishings and art, as well as the careful landscaping that surrounds it.

The headquarters building is arranged in two separate groupings of offices which are linked by a central atrium. The large skylit space in the atrium provides the facility's architectural and social focus and serves as the main entrance to the headquarters complex, welcoming visitors to the company. The building's circulation focuses on the atrium's escalators and bridges, which bring employees together in a setting that is at once vital and serene.

Primary materials for the building are a warm red brick, creamy yellow limestone, terra cotta, pale green glass and teakwood trim. Polished yellow metal provides an accent. These materials were selected to symbolize the company's connections to the land. Drawing from the American tradition of rural craft, special furnishings complement the natural materials of the systems furniture that are used throughout the open office areas. Maple and cherry woods frame private offices and special facilities. Artworks inspired by agricultural themes and recurring pattern motifs that emphasize cereals and grains are used throughout the offices. Overall, the atmosphere is one of light and warmth.

(*right*) *Site plan.*
(*p.85*) *Landscaping with ha-ha walls on the west side of the building.*
(*pp.86–87*) *Kellogg's main entrance.*
Photos (*pp.84–91*) *except p.90 and p.91 bottom by George Cott.*
Photos of p.90 and p.91 bottom by HOK Photography.

(右) 配置図.
(p.85) 西側からみる．手前は隠れ垣のある庭園.
(p.86-87) メイン・エントランスを見る.

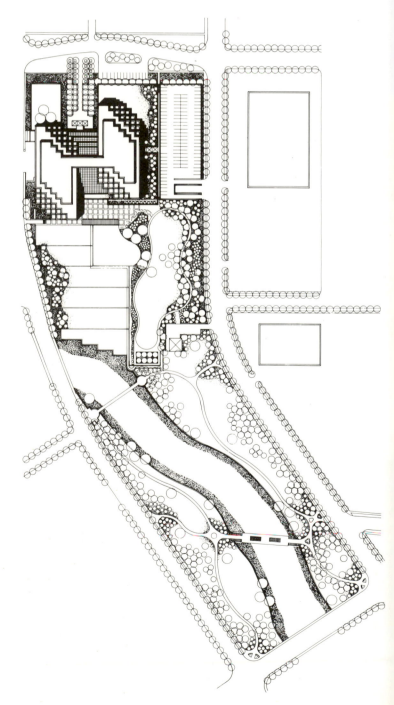

世界的な食品会社であるケロッグ社は新本社に経営部門を統合する必要を生じ，会社の活動の根源にある価値感を建築によって表現したいと考えた．HOKは，バトル・クリークのダウンタウンにある小さな公園を見渡す17エーカーの土地に，見晴らしのよい優雅な本社施設を建設することを提案した．

その敷地は再開発の必要に迫られていたが，そこに建設することをケロッグが決定したことは，ケロッグ社創設地の市民に対して，再開発の確約と感謝をともに表すこととなった．本社敷地を貫流するバトル・クリーク川の一部を整備するための連邦政府の許可を得るに際しても，HOKはケロッグ社およびバトル・クリーク市の積極的な協力者として働いた．

アメリカの農業地帯の基本的な価値観がケロッグ社の経営哲学にも大きく寄与しているため，この本社ビルは土地を守る尊い仕事と農業文化に対する尊敬をあらゆる方法で表現している．建物の低層でセットバックしてゆく姿から，ケロッグ社の意図した主題をもった調度品や美術品，あるいは周囲の念入りな造園に至るまで，施設のあらゆるところにその証を見出すことができる．

この本社ビルは二つのオフィス・グループに分けられ，中央アトリウムで結ばれている．天空光を採り入れたアトリウムの広い空間は，施設の建築的および社会的中心であり，ここを訪れる人々を迎え入れる本社ビルのメイン・エントランスとなっている．この建物の動線はアトリウムのエスカレータとブリッジに集中しており，社員たちは活気と静謐を兼ね備えた環境で働けるようになっている．

建物のおもな材料は暖かみのある赤の煉瓦，クリーム・イエローの石灰岩，テラコッタ，薄緑のガラス，そしてチークの枠材である．光沢のある黄銅がアクセントを添えている．これらの素材はこの地域とケロッグ社との結び付きを象徴するために選ばれた．

アメリカの農村工芸の伝統をもとにした独特な調度が，広々としたオフィス全体に用いられ，システム家具の天然素材が互いに補完しあっている．楓と桜がプライヴェート・オフィスと特別施設を強調し，農業的主題を想起させる美術品や穀物を強調したパターン・モティーフが，オフィスのあらゆるところに用いられている．全体的に，明るく暖かい雰囲気である．

(right top) Fifih floor plan.
(right middle) Ground floor plan.
(right bottom) Section.
(p.89) Main entrance at twilight.

（右上）5階平面図．
（右中）1階平面図．
（右下）断面図．
（p.89）メイン・エントランス夜景．

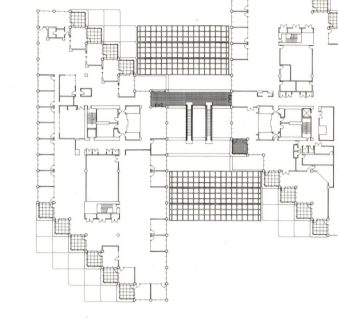

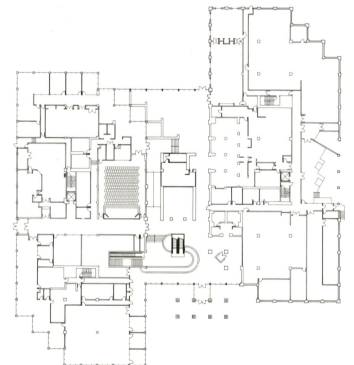

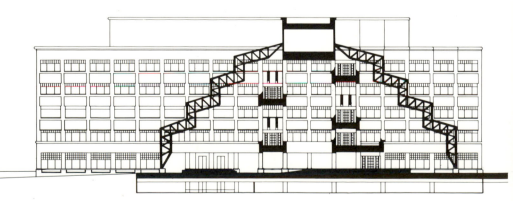

(p.90) *View of atrium from second level bridge.*
(top) *Doorway detail viewed from atrium bridge.*
(above) *Waiting area.*

（p.90）　ブリッジから見たアトリウム.
（上）アトリウムのブリッジからの入口.
（下）待合室.

Fairmont Hotel, San Jose

San Jose, California, USA

サンノゼ・フェアモント・ホテル
アメリカ，カリフォルニア州サンノゼ
1987

Taking their inspiration from the other grand hotels of the world, the Fairmont Hotels offer an atmosphere of first-class luxury. The 583-room Fairmont Hotel in San Jose is a significant element of a multi-block, downtown redevelopment project. Because of the importance placed on revitalizing the neighborhood, the hotel's design emphasizes easy access to, through and around the facility with an exterior pedestrian arcade and a lobby plan that encourages pedestrian traffic.

The hotel, a steel-frame structure, is finished in rose-hued, granite-aggregate precast concrete with polished-granite accents and copper roofing. Stylistically, it is reminiscent of Spanish colonial architecture. In addition to guest rooms, the facility contains two ballrooms, meetings rooms, restaurants, shops, and a health club. To reduce the impact of the building's size, the San Jose Fairmont steps back in two stages. A rooftop pool and guest cabanas cap the lower level and overlook a nearby park.

フェアモント・ホテルは，世界の他の豪華ホテルの影響を受けて，一流の贅沢な雰囲気を漂わせている。

583室をもつサンノゼ・フェアモント・ホテルは，多区画に渡るダウンタウン再開発プロジェクトの重要な要素となっている。近隣活性化ということから，ホテルの設計は，戸外のアーケードやロビーなどからホテルの各所に歩行者が入り易いという点に重点がおかれている。

ホテルは鉄骨構造で，ばら色の花崗岩粒の混ざったプレキャスト・コンクリートを用い，アクセントとして研磨仕上げの花崗岩が施されており，屋根は銅葺きである。様式的には，スペインのコロニアル建築を想起させる。客室の他に，二つの宴会場，会議室，レストラン，売店，ヘルス・クラブなどがある。サンノゼ・フェアモント・ホテルは，建物の大きさの圧迫感を軽減するため，2層にステップ・バックしている。低層部の屋上はプールと客用更衣室があって，近くの公園を見渡せる。

(*right top*) Site plan.
(*right middle*) Typical tower level plan.
(*right bottom*) Lobby level plan.
(*p.93*) Main tower and bay.
(*pp.94-95*) General view from the City Plaza Park.
Photos (*pp.92-97*)
by George Cott.

（右上）配置図。
（右中）タワー棟客室平面図。
（右下）ロビー階平面図。
（p.93）タワー客室棟と東南側の半円形の突出し。
（p.94-95）シティ・プラザ・パークから見た全景。

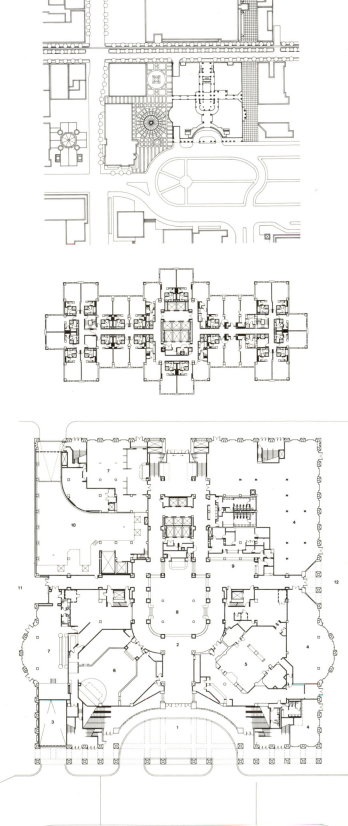

Legend
1-Auto court
2-Ground lobby
3-Parking entry
4-Retail
5-Gourmet restaurant
6-Meeting／dining room
7-Restaurant
8-Lobby bar
9-Front desk
10-Service／receiving
11-Plaza
12-Paseo de San Antonio

0 10 25   50

(*above*) *Entrance to First Street*.
(*p.97*) *Lobby*.

（上）ファースト・ストリート側入口．
(p.97) ロビー．

Fairmont Hotel, Chicago

with Fujikawa Johnson and Associates, Inc.
Chicago, Illinois, USA

シカゴ・フェアモント・ホテル
アメリカ，イリノイ州シカゴ

1988

The 45-story Fairmont Hotel in Chicago is located on a prime site at Illinois Center, giving hotel guests commanding views of Chicago's famous Loop, Lake Michigan or Grant Park.

The Chicago Fairmont's solid profile rises from a richly detailed base to a tower articulated by bay windows and capped by a turret. The 700-room hotel is clad in rose-hued granite and topped with a roof of pale green copper, emphasizing the Fairmont's warmth in contrast to its businesslike neighbors.

The richly finished lobby, further embellished by a formal staircase, is distinguished by its octagonal floorplan. The registration desk, restaurants and retail shops surround the central conversation lounge.

45階建てのシカゴのフェアモント・ホテルは，イリノイ・センターの一等地に位置し，客は，有名なシカゴのループやミシガン湖，グラント・パークなどの景観を楽しむことができる．

シカゴ・フェアモント・ホテルは，ディテールの豊かな基部から，出窓でポイントをつけ，小塔をかぶせたタワーとして立ち上がっている．700室のホテルの表面はばら色の花崗岩で装われ，頂部は薄緑色の銅で屋根が葺いてあり，周囲のビジネス風の雰囲気と対照を成してフェアモントの暖かさを強調している．

贅沢な仕上げのロビーは，格調高い階段でさらに光彩を増しながら，その八角形のフロアによって際立ったものになっている．そして中央の談話ラウンジを囲んで，フロント・デスク，レストラン，売店などがある．

(*right top*) Site plan.
(*right middle*) Typical guest floor plan.
(*right bottom*) Lobby level plan.
(*p.99*) View from across Lakeshore Drive.
Photos (*p.98-103*) by George Cott.

（右上）配置図．
（右中）客室基準階平面図．
（右下）ロビー階平面図．
(p.99)レイクショア・ドライヴ越しに見る．

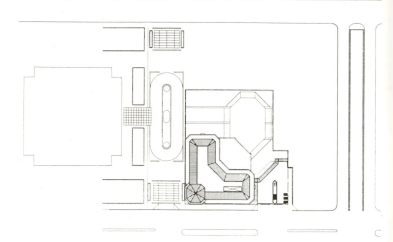

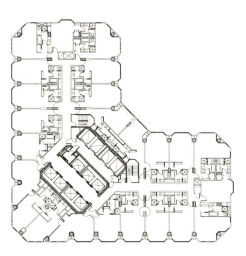

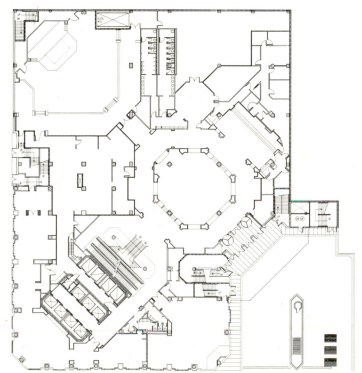

(*above*) *South side of the hotel, with entry portico at right.*
(*p.101*) *Window detail.*

（上）南側をみる．右手に入口のポルティコが見える．
（p.101）窓・壁面詳細．

(above) The grand stairway in the lobby.
(p.102) Lobby.

（上）ロビーの大階段.
（p.102）ロビー.

Burger King Corporation World Headquarters

Miami, Florida, USA

バーガー・キング社世界本社
アメリカ，フロリダ州マイアミ
1987

Lively exteriors of pink and gray, modulated by landscaped terraces, set the tone for the Burger King Corporation World Headquarters, home to a young and growing company that wanted a dynamic headquarters to reflect its energetic workforce. The campus-style setting brings together several corporate facilities on a site that emphasizes and incorporates the region's natural beauty.

The Burger King Corporation World Headquarters consists of four structures: a four-story office building, a two-story conference and training center, a two-story research and development facility, and a two-story computer center. Because of the possibility of hurricanes, all buildings are elevated 22 feet above grade as protection from storm surges. Two levels of parking are placed underneath the office building.

The 130-acre site on the shore of Biscayne Bay is located 15 miles south of Miami. It is nestled between stands of endangered white pine, mangrove and native oak forests, and contained a nine-acre lake which was been integrated in the final design.

The central lobby of the office building, a glass-front atrium containing escalators and fountains, provides the main focus for the buildings. The office building sets the tone for the rest of the facility, with a waterfront orientation that retreats in a series of stepped terraces which are shaded and planted to enhance the appreciation of the surrounding environment.

The buildings are clad in pale rose precast concrete scored with crosshatching and punctuated by insets of green marble. Inside, light-colored woods, white walls and turquoise carpeting recall a traditional Florida palette. Many large windows, of varying designs and types of glass, provide different qualities of natural light and views of the outdoors from nearly every room.

While more formal landscaping prevails in the immediate vicinity of the buildings, much of the Burger King Corporation World Headquarters site intentionally has been left in its natural state. In several areas, vegetation has been thinned to enhance the growth of native species, and the banks of the lake, recently stocked with fish, have been sloped to encourage congregations of water fowl.

The entire site has been designed to encourage its use by employees, and includes a wide variety of recreational facilities. Amenities include an art gallery, weight-training room, aerobics studio, volleyball pit, and baseball fields. One cafeteria serves the entire complex and, like other special facilities, it faces the lake.

(right) Site plan.
(p.105) View across water to Burger King complex, from the north. Burger King University is visible on the left end.
Photos (pp.105-112) by George Cott.
Photos (p.113) by Cervin Robinson.

(右) 配置図．
(p.105)池を隔てて北側から見る．左端にはバーガー・キング大学が見える．

0 50 100 200 400

植栽の施されたテラスに合わせて，バーガー・キング社世界本社の外壁は生き生きとしたピンクとグレーの色調でまとめられている．この本社屋は成長過程にある若い企業の帰るべき我が家であり，そのエネルギッシュな社員たちの意気を反映するダイナミックな建物でなければならなかった．キャンパス風に計画することによって，会社の各施設がこの地域の自然の美しさを生かしながら，あるいは強調しながら敷地内にまとめられている．

バーガー・キング社世界本社は四つの建物から成る．すなわち，4階建てのオフィス・ビル，2階建ての研修訓練センター，2階建ての研究開発施設，および2階建てのコンピュータ・センターである．ハリケーンが襲ってくることを考慮して，すべての建物は暴風や大波に備えて地上22フィートの高架式になっており，2層の駐車場がオフィス・ビルの下にある．

ビスケーン湾の砂浜にあるこの130エーカーの敷地はマイアミの南15マイルのところに位置し，絶滅の危機に瀕したストローブ松とマングローブと自生するオークの森に囲まれ，最終計画の段階で取り入れられた9エーカーの湖もある．オフィス・ビルの中央ロビーは正面がガラス張りのアトリウムで，エスカレータと噴水があり，建物群の中心を成している．また，周囲の環境を十分楽しめるよう日除けがあり植栽のある，段状に後退してゆくテラスがウォーター・フロント志向を表現していて，このオフィス・ビルが他の施設の佇まいにも影響を与えている．

建物の外壁仕上げは，格子組みの緑色の大理石模様をアクセントにした薄ばら色のプレキャスト・コンクリートである．内部は明るい色の木材と白い壁とターコイズ・ブルーのカーペットが，伝統的なフロリダ風の配色を想起させる．各種様々な形のガラスを用いた大きな窓がたくさんあり，自然光が様々に変化されて採り入れられており，ほとんど全室から外の景色が眺められる．

建物のごく周辺は造園が施されているが，バーガー・キング社世界本社の敷地の多くは，意図的に自然の状態を残している．いくつかの場所では，自生の種の成長を促すため植生をまばらにしているところもあり，また，最近，魚が放流された湖では土手をスロープにして水鳥が集まりやすくしている．

敷地全体にわたって，従業員の利用の便をはかるよう計画され，いろいろなレクリエーション施設が整えられている．そういった施設には，アート・ギャラリーやウェイト・トレーニング室，エアロビクス・スタジオ，バレーボール・コート，野球場などがある．カフェテリアは全施設に供せられ，他の特別施設と同様に湖に面している．

(pp.106-107) Boardwalk edging the water in front of the Burger King complex, viewed from the southeast.
(below) West elevation of Burger King Training Center.
(middle) West elevation.
(bottom) East elevation.
(p.109) The Burger King Training Center makes up the west side of the complex. Palm trees line the drive to the main entry.

(p.106-107) 歩行デッキから見た東側の構成．
（下上）バーガー・キング・トレーニング・センター西側立面図．
（下中）西側立面図．
（下）東側立面図．
(p.109) 西側のバーガー・キング・トレーニング・センター．椰子の並木のある通りから主玄関に至る．

(from top to bottom)
Sixth floor plan.
Fourth floor plan.
Third floor plan.
Ground parking floor plan.

（上）6階平面図.
（中上）4階平面図.
（中下）3階平面図.
（下）1階駐車場階平面図.

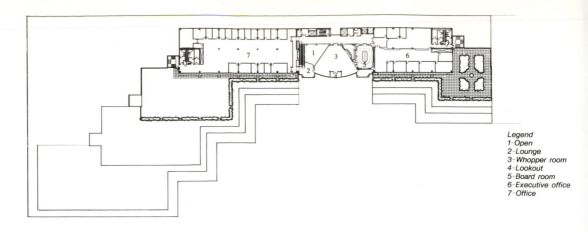

Legend
1-Open
2-Lounge
3-Whopper room
4-Lookout
5-Board room
6-Executive office
7-Office

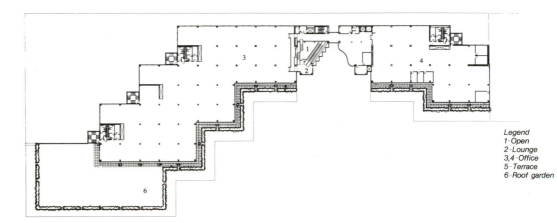

Legend
1-Open
2-Lounge
3,4-Office
5-Terrace
6-Roof garden

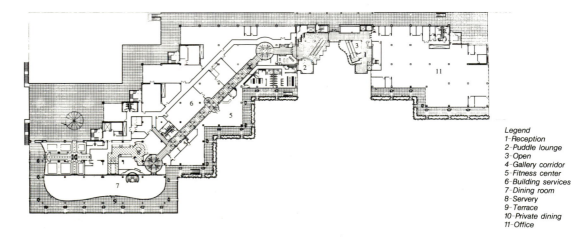

Legend
1-Reception
2-Puddle lounge
3-Open
4-Gallery corridor
5-Fitness center
6-Building services
7-Dining room
8-Servery
9-Terrace
10-Private dining
11-Office

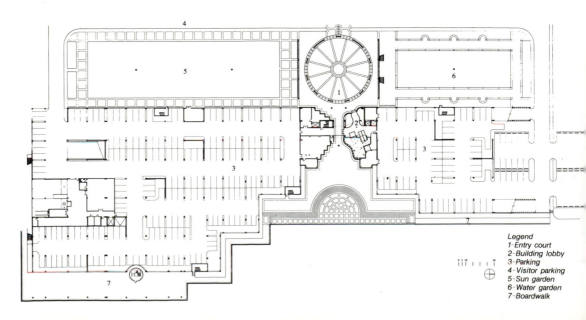

Legend
1-Entry court
2-Building lobby
3-Parking
4-Visitor parking
5-Sun garden
6-Water garden
7-Boardwalk

(top) View of entry drive.
(above) Twilight view across interior courtyard.

（上）西側の入口前庭へのアプローチ.
（下）入口前庭夜景.

(p.112) Escalators in atrium area.
(top) Waiting area at top of escalator.
(above) Board room.

（p.112）アトリウムのエスカレータ.
（上）アトリウム上部の待合室.
（下）役員会議室.

World Bank "J" Building

Washington, D.C., USA

世界銀行「J」ビルディング
アメリカ，ワシントンD. C.
1987

Located on a prominent, corner site in Washington, D.C.'s financial district, just a few blocks from the White House, the World Bank "J" Building needed to relate to the style and manner of its traditional, business-like neighbors. But World Bank officials requested a less traditional interior arrangement, with as many offices as possible having access to natural light.

In its strongly horizontal configuration, the World Bank "J" Building reflects the style of neighboring buildings. Rounded corners heighten the horizontal impression, while deepset window openings add texture and interest. Salmon-colored granite cladding, and matching precast concrete on the upper floors, complement the financial district's palette of tan-gray limestones, granites, and concretes. The exterior impression of the building, says the *Washington Post*, carries "a certain authority, as if it had been there for years."

But the World Bank "J" Building's floor plan is far from traditional. It is organized around two atriums that extend from the third to the 11th floors and are varied by occasional bridges and terraces. Besides supplying occupants with daylight, the atriums also clearly orient visitors within the building. Light flows into the atriums from skylights on the roof and two large, convex windows that interrupt the west facade, without diminishing the building's sense of scale. The structural plan of 40-by-40-foot typical bays provides large column-free interior spaces not generally found in financial-district office buildings. Adding to the building's flexibility and efficiency are six-inch raised floors to facilitate communication and data access throughout the building.

A mix of open and closed offices prevails, with glazed clerestories supplying closed offices with natural light. Non-reflective, energy-efficient glass has been used throughout. In combination with the atriums and a centrally controlled lighting system, designers hope to produce a 40-percent energy savings.

The 400,000-square-foot "J" Building also contains a conference center and two levels of below-grade parking. It is connected to the main World Bank complex, which is located across the street, by means of an underground tunnel.

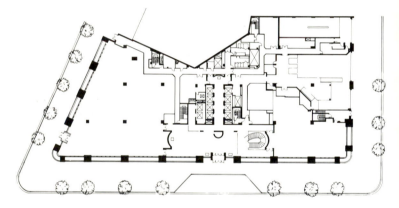

世界銀行「J」ビルディングは，その水平的要素を強調した外観においては周辺の建物と類似している．隅部の丸みは水平感を強め，一方，深く引き込んだ窓が全体としての基調に味わいを添えている．サーモン・ピンクの花崗岩の外装とそれに調和した上層階のプレキャスト・コンクリートが，黄灰色の石灰岩や花崗岩，コンクリートといった金融街の配色を補完している．このビルの外観の印象を，「あたかも長年そこに建っているかのようなある種の威厳を漂わせている」とワシントン・ポストは評している．

しかし，世界銀行「J」ビルディングの平面計画は，まったく伝統的な形からはかけ離れている．3階から11階まで吹き抜ける二つのアトリウムの周囲に各フロアが配置され，適宜ブリッジやテラスを設けて変化をつけており，アトリウムはビルのテナントに日光をもたらすだけでなく，訪問者にもビル内での位置をつかみやすくさせている．光はスカイライトと西面にある二つの曲面になったガラス窓を通してアトリウムに入る．

標準柱間を40×40フィートとする構造計画によって，金融街のオフィス・スペースには通常見られない，自由な広い内部空間が生み出されている．さらに，建物の融通性と効率性に加えて，6インチ高めた床によってビル全体のコミュニケーションとデータ・アクセスが容易になっている．オープン・オフィスと個別オフィスとの混合がうまく組み合されており，個別オフィスはガラス張りの高窓から自然光が入るようになっている．

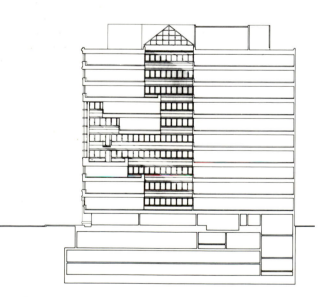

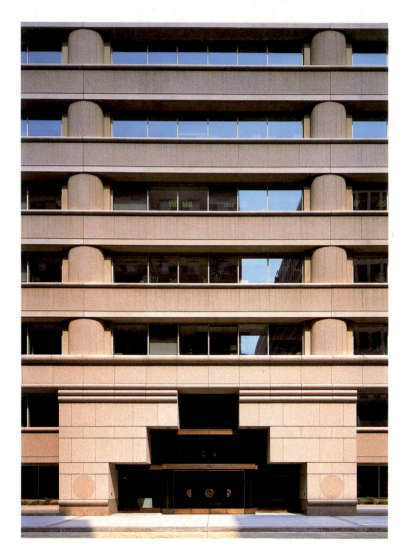

(p.114 from top to bottom.)
Typical floor plan.
Site/ground floor plan.
Section.
(p.115) Looking northeast
along 18th Street.
(above) Main entrance on
18th Street.
(p.117) Night view.
Photos (pp.115–119) by
George Cott.

（p.114　上から下に）
基準階平面図.
配置・1階平面図
断面図
（p.115）18番街沿いに北東から見る. 自然
光を採り入れる二つの大きなガラスの曲
面が見える.
（上）18番街入口正面.
（p.117）夜景.

(p.118) Formal seating and landscaping in an atrium space.
(top) Looking down from a pedestrian bridge to the offices surrounding one of the atrium spaces.
(above) The entry lobby.

(p.118)アトリウム. 花崗岩のベンチや植栽が施されている.
(上) 事務室で囲まれたアトリウム.
(下) 玄関ロビー.

Joe Robbie Stadium

Dade County, Florida, USA

ジョー・ロビー・スタジアム
アメリカ，フロリダ州デード郡
1987

HOK's Kansas City, Missouri, office specializes in the design of sports facilities. Some recently completed facilities include the Bradley Center Arena, Joe Robbie Stadium and Pilot Field. Projects to be built include the Camden Yards Twin-Stadium Complex, as well as a number of other sports facilities throughout the United States and in Europe. As of fall 1989, HOK was chief architect for all but one stadium under construction in the United States.
Joe Robbie Stadium is a 75,000-seat, open-air stadium that is home to the Miami Dolphins football team.
In 1989, it was the site for the Super Bowl. In addition to field level and upper deck spectator seating, Joe Robbie has 216 luxury suites and 10,000 club-level seats, which are connected to a specially designed lounge that encircles the stadium.

ミズーリ州の HOK カンサス・シティ事務所は，スポーツ施設を専門に設計している．最近完成したものに，ブラッドレー・センター・アリーナ，ジョー・ロビー・スタジアム，パイロット・フィールドなどがある．これから建設されるプロジェクトとしては，カムデン・ヤーズ・ツイン・スタジアムをはじめ，全米やヨーロッパの多くのスポーツ施設が予定されている．1989年秋現在，HOK は，アメリカで建設中のスタジアムのうちひとつを除いて残り全部の主任建築家であった．

ジョー・ロビー・スタジアムは7万5,000席の野外スタジアムで，フットボール・チーム，マイアミ・ドルフィンズのホーム・スタジアムである．1989年には，スーパー・ボウルがここで行われた．フィールドと同じ高さ，および上方デッキの観客席に加え，216のデラックス席と，1万席のクラブ・レヴェルの観客席があり，そこからはスタジアムを取り囲む特別設計のラウンジにゆくことができる．

(right top) Suite/club seating reference plan.
(right bottom) Site plan.
(p.121) View of spectator seating from the field.
(pp.122-123) Stadium in the midst of the football game.
Photos (p.120-125) by HOK Photography.

（右上）特別席平面図．
（右下）配置図．
（p.121）グラウンドから観客席をみる．
（p.122-123）フットボールの試合中のスタジアム．

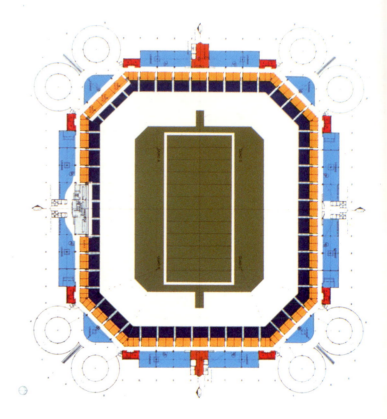

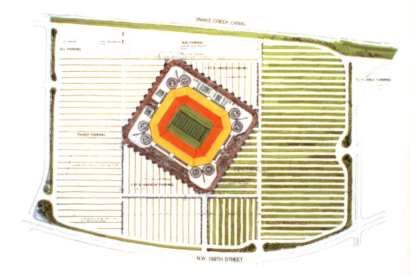

(p.124) *View from the pedestrian slope.*
(top) *Aerial View.*
(above) *View of the entrance facade.*

(p.124) 歩行用スロープからみる.
(上) 全景.
(下) 入口側のファサード.

Bradley Center Arena

with Venture Architects
Milwaukee, Wisconsin, USA

ブラッドレー・センター・アリーナ
アメリカ，ウィスコンシン州ミルウォーキー
1988

Bradley Center is a 20,000-seat multipurpose sports and entertainment arena that emphasizes amenities and spectator comfort. The arena has 68 private box suites. Its three-concourse design puts all food service facilities, restrooms and exits within easy access of every seating area.

ブラッドレー・センターは，快適さと観衆の居心地のよさに力を入れたスポーツと娯楽のための2万席の多目的アリーナである．このアリーナにはプライヴェート・ボックス席が68ある．三つのコンコースのある設計で，どの位置の席からも，フード・サーヴィスの売店，手洗い，出入口などに簡単にゆけるように考えられている．

(below) Site plan (level 100). (p.127) Arena in the midst of the basketball match. Photos (pp.126–131) by HOK Photography.

（下）配置図（レヴェル100）．
(p.127) バスケットボールの試合が行われているアリーナ．

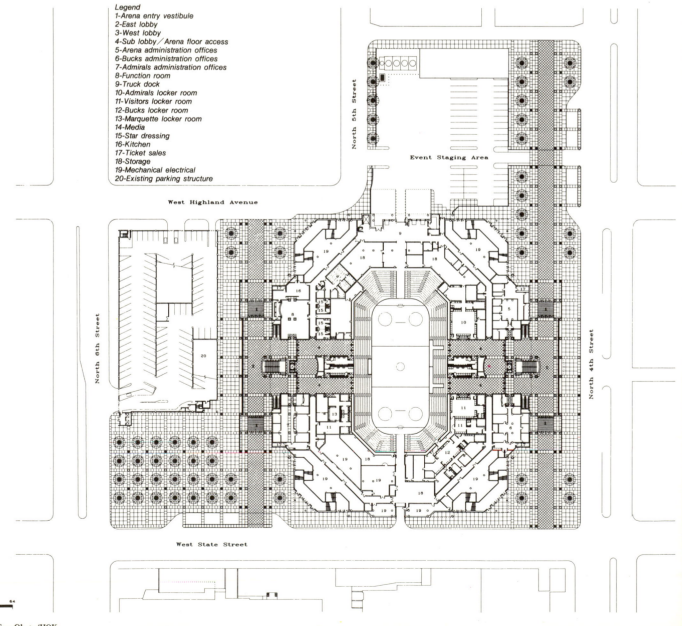

Legend
1-Arena entry vestibule
2-East lobby
3-West lobby
4-Sub lobby／Arena floor access
5-Arena administration offices
6-Bucks administration offices
7-Admirals administration offices
8-Function room
9-Truck dock
10-Admirals locker room
11-Visitors locker room
12-Bucks locker room
13-Marquette locker room
14-Media
15-Star dressing
16-Kitchen
17-Ticket sales
18-Storage
19-Mechanical electrical
20-Existing parking structure

North 5th Street

Event Staging Area

West Highland Avenue

North 6th Street

North 4th Street

West State Street

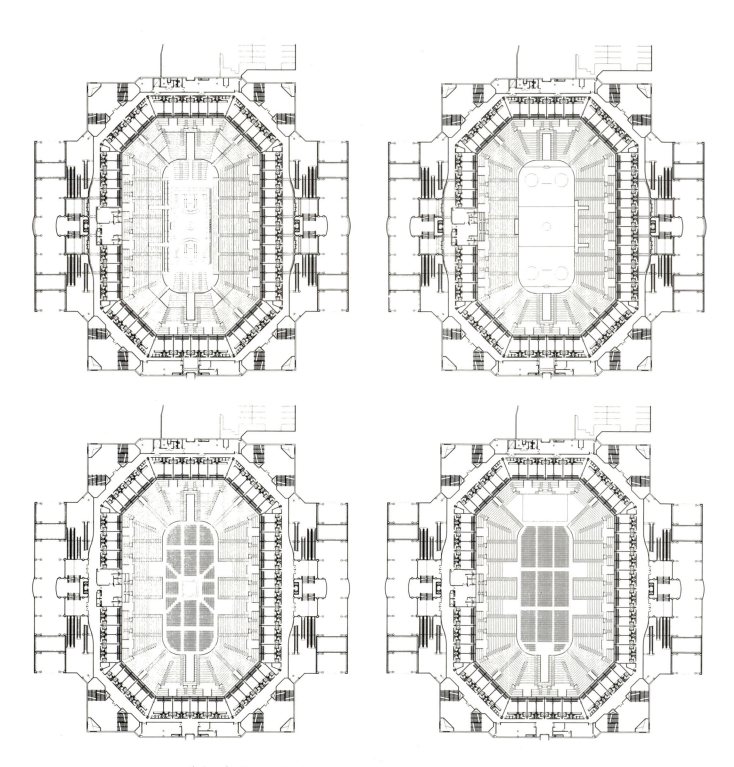

(*above*) *Event Configurations*：
(*top left*) *Basketball*.
(*top right*) *Hockey*.
(*bottom left*) *Center stage*.
(*bottom right*) *End stage*.
(*p.129*) *Lobby*.
(*pp.130-131*) *General view from the southeast*.

（上）アリーナ・ヴァリエーション：
（左上）バスケットボール.
（右上）ホッケイ.
（左下）中央舞台型.
（右下）端部舞台型.
（p.129）ロビー.
（p.130-131）東南からみた全景.

Pilot Field

Buffalo, New York, USA

パイロット・フィールド
アメリカ，ニューヨーク州バッファロー
1988

Pilot Field is a 19,000-seat baseball stadium that hosts AAA League games, and can be expanded to 40,000 seats if the city attracts a major league team. Pilot Field was designed to conform with neighboring historic buildings, with features such as arched window openings, decorative grillwork, and inset marble panels.

パイロット・フィールドは，３Ａリーグの試合を行う１万9,000席のベースボール・スタジアムで，メジャー・リーグをこの町に誘致できれば，４万席に拡張されることになっている．パイロット・フィールドの設計は，周囲の歴史的建築物と調和するように考えられており，アーチ形の窓や装飾をほどこした格子窓，大理石のはめ込み板などに特徴がある．

(pp.132-133) *View from the east. Lake Erie is visible on the background.*
(above) *View from the Washington Street on the west.*
(p.135) *View of the facade on the Swan Street.*
Photos (pp.132-137) by HOK Photography.

(p.132-133)東側から見る．背景にエリー湖がみえる．
(上) 西側のワシントン通りから見る．
(p.135) スワン通り側のファサード．

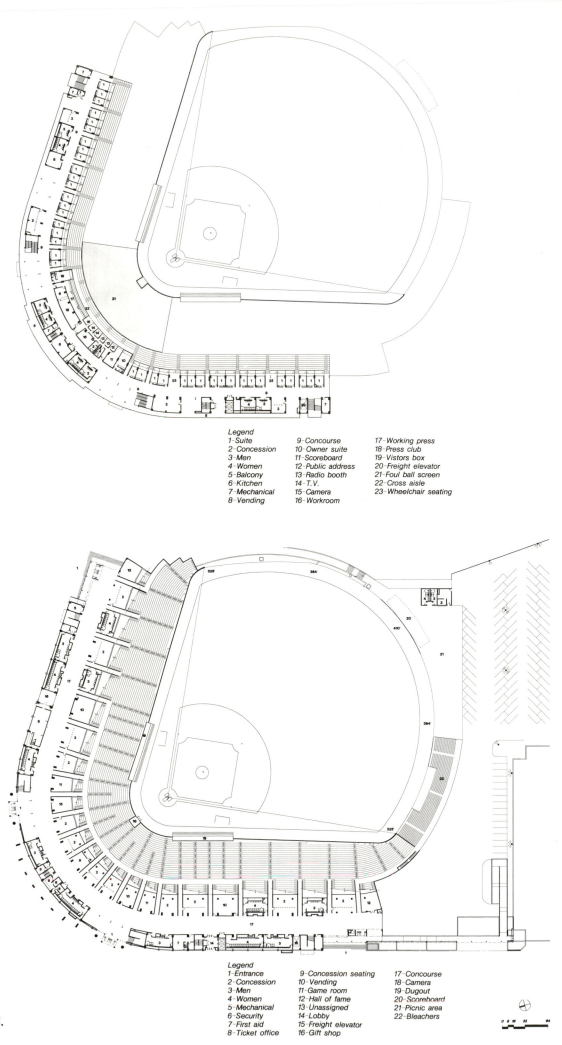

Legend
1-Suite
2-Concession
3-Men
4-Women
5-Balcony
6-Kitchen
7-Mechanical
8-Vending
9-Concourse
10-Owner suite
11-Scoreboard
12-Public address
13-Radio booth
14-T.V.
15-Camera
16-Workroom
17-Working press
18-Press club
19-Vistors box
20-Freight elevator
21-Foul ball screen
22-Cross aisle
23-Wheelchair seating

(right top) Club level plan.
*(right bottom) Main concourse
level plan.*

（上）クラブ・レヴェル平面図.
（下）メイン・コンコース・レヴェル平面図.

Legend
1-Entrance
2-Concession
3-Men
4-Women
5-Mechanical
6-Security
7-First aid
8-Ticket office
9-Concession seating
10-Vending
11-Game room
12-Hall of fame
13-Unassigned
14-Lobby
15-Freight elevator
16-Gift shop
17-Concourse
18-Camera
19-Dugout
20-Scoreboard
21-Picnic area
22-Bleachers

(*top*) *View of the arcade.*　　（上）アーチをもったアーケード.
(*above*) *View of the entrance.*　　（下）入口を見る.

Kansai International Airport Design Competition

with Kajima Corporation
Osaka, Japan
関西国際空港旅客ターミナルビル設計競技案
協同：鹿島建設（岡島毅・由里知久・坂本弘之）
大阪
1988

To be constructed on manmade Airport Island is Osaka Bay, the Kansai International Airport and Aero City is intended to be both a domestic hub and international gateway.   This design, submitted in competition, was not the winning selection.

A main terminal and two satellite terminals form the basis of the design, symbolizing flight through their triangular composition. This arrangement consolidates the flow of travelers and contributes to the efficient movement of cargo and aircraft. The clustering of airline terminals and the use of below-grade people-movers to connect each of the satellite terminals to the main terminal also contributes to the efficiency of the design.

This design for Kansai Airport is also distinguished by its emphasis on natural lighting, the main source of which is a three-story atrium that runs the length of the main terminal building. Clerestories at the juncture of structural bays in the tension-roof design also admit light.

大阪湾に浮かぶ人工飛行場に建設される関西国際空港およびエアロ・シティは，国内線の中心であると同時に，世界への玄関になることも目的として建設されるものである．しかし，設計競技に提出された HOK＋鹿島建設チームのこの案は，採用案とはならなかった．

メイン・ターミナルと二つのサテライト・ターミナルが，計画の基本を形づくっており，その三角形の構成が飛行を象徴している．この配置は搭乗客の流れを統一し，貨物や航空機の効率的な移動を可能にする．航空会社のターミナルを集中させ，各サテライト・ターミナルとメイン・ターミナルとを結んだ地下のピープル・ムーヴァーの使用も，この計画に盛り込まれた効率性という点に貢献している．

この関西国際空港計画のもう一つの優れた点は，自然光を重視したことである．メイン・ターミナルビルの長さいっぱいに伸びた3層吹抜けのアトリウムが主となって，自然光を導入している．さらに，テンション・ルーフの設計においては構造ベイ連結部の明かり取りからも光が入るように設計されている．

(below) Domestic arrival/ departure level plan (scale 1: 4000).
(bottom) Level B1 plan (scale 1: 4000).
(p.139) View of the entrance road and domestic arrival/departure lobby.
(pp.140–141) General view. Photos by the courtesy of Kajima Corporation.

（上）国内線出発・到着ロビー階平面図：縮尺 1/4000.
（下）地階平面図.
(p.139) 入口前のアプローチ道路より出発・到着ロビーをみる.
(p.140-141) 全景.

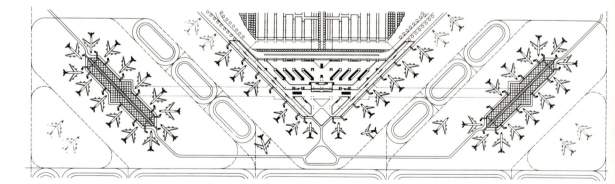

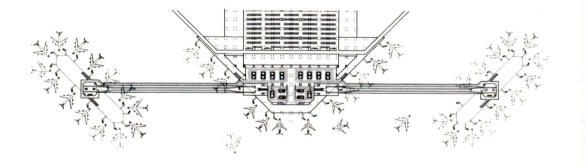

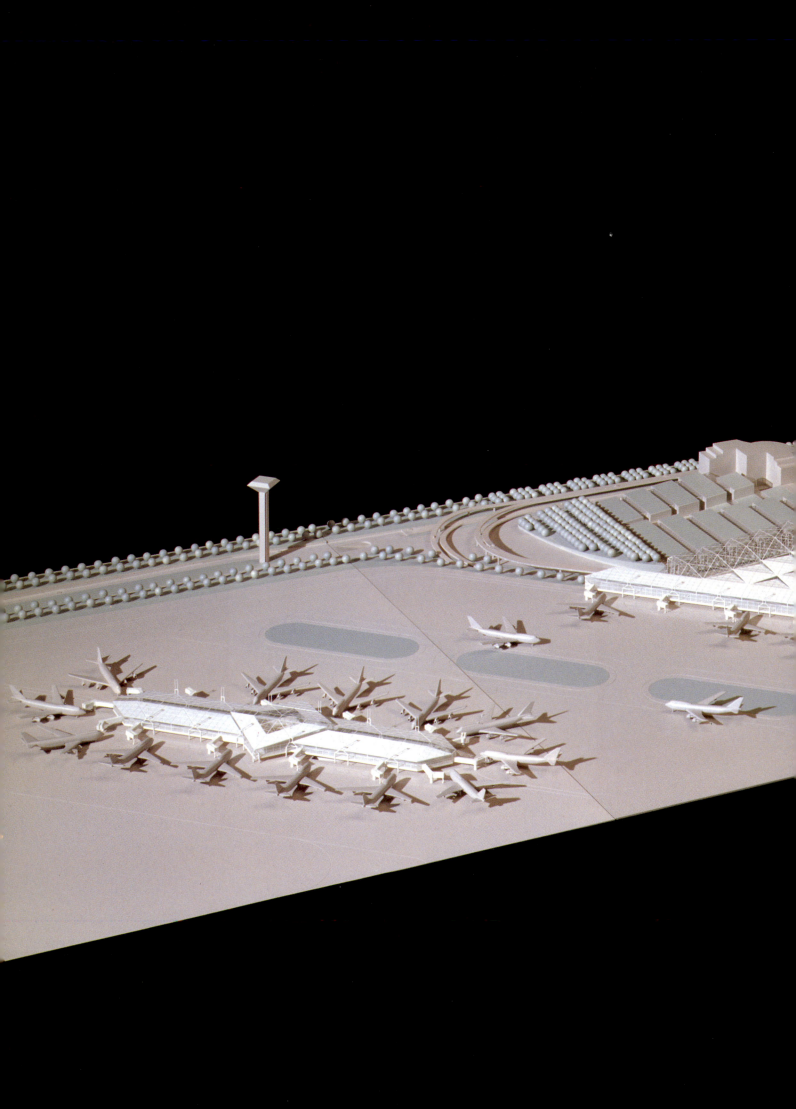

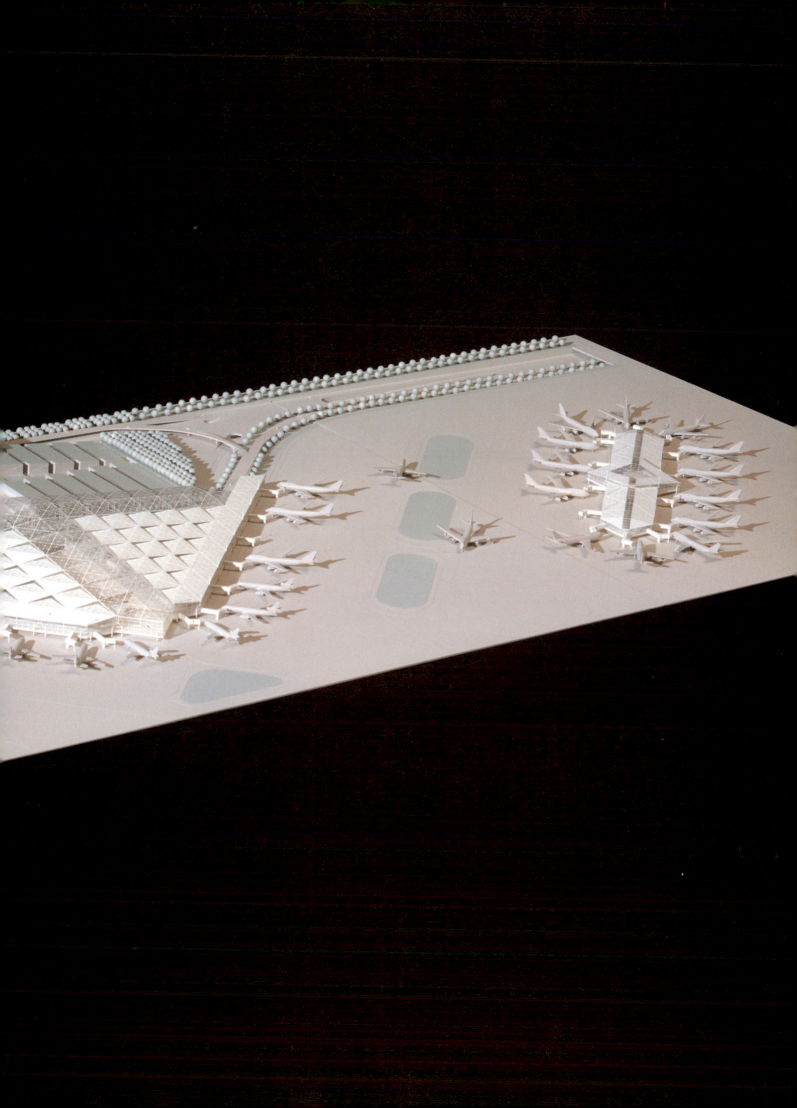

Metropolitan Square

St. Louis, Missouri, USA

メトロポリタン・スクエア・オフィス・タワー
アメリカ，ミズーリ州セントルイス

1989

The tallest building on the St. Louis skyline, the 42-story
Metropolitan Square is also the single largest office building ever
developed on a speculative basis by the Metropolitan Life Insurance
Company. Its design strategy reflects a dual approach: to visibly
demonstrate a kinship with the St. Louis cityscape while
distinguishing itself as a luxury skyscraper.

The building's profile celebrates the classic era of urban skyscrapers
and pays tribute to the renaissance of downtown St. Louis. Its
50-foot-high lobby, finished in marble, granite and brass, recalls the
grandeur of great 20th century skyscrapers. The lobby's marble walls
are topped by two large murals: a two-panel mural near the main
entrance depicts the city's past and present, and a seven-panel mural
titled "An Urban Odyssey" illustrates a day in the life of a city
worker.

Metropolitan Square is clad in a gold/bronze granite complemented
by large expanses of similarly colored glass, giving the building a
sleek, contemporary look. Strong vertical elements, emphasized by
deep setbacks, slim the tower's profile.

The tower's seven-story granite base, which conceals parking for
approximately 1,000 vehicles, opens on one side to a pedestrian
plaza. It is surrounded by a covered arcade that welcomes pedestrian
traffic to the 18,500 square feet of retail/restaurant space
surrounding the lobby.

A two-story, glass-enclosed penthouse, capped by a gabled
coppertoned roof, tops the tower. Metropolitan Square's peaked
roofline is dramatically spotlighted at night to draw attention to the
downtown skyline and to reference "The Light That Never Fails," a
beacon of the roof of the Met Life building in New York City which
has become the company's signature.

セントルイスで最も高い42階建てのメトロポリタン・スクエアは，メトロポリ
タン生命保険会社のオフィス・ビルの中では最大のものでもある．それ自体豪
華な摩天楼として際立ちながら，同時にセントルイスの都市景観に調和するこ
と．この二重のアプローチはこのビルの設計戦略を反映したものである．
建物の姿は，都市のスカイスクレイパーという古典的時代の良さを具えながら，
しかもダウンタウン・セントルイスへの心配りも忘れてはいない．大理石と花
崗岩そして真鍮で仕上げられた高さ50フィートのロビーは，偉大なる20世紀の
摩天楼の壮観さを想起させる．ロビーの大理石壁の上部には2幅の壁画がある．
メイン・エントランス近くには市の過去と現在を描いた2枚構成の壁画で，も
うひとつは「アーバン・オデュッセイア」と題された7枚構成の壁画で，都市
生活者の一日の生活が描かれている．
メトロポリタン・スクエアの外装は金色あるいはブロンズ色の花崗岩と，それ
と同色のガラス面で構成されている．また奥行きの深いセットバックで強調さ
れた力強い垂直的要素がタワーを細く見せている．
タワーの7層の花崗岩の基壇部分は，片側を歩行者広場に開放した形になって
いて，地下に1,000台収容の駐車場がある．その周囲は屋根付きアーケードにな
っており，ロビーを囲む1万8,500平方フィートの店舗とレストランに人々を招
き入れる．タワーの頂上には，切妻型の緑青色の屋根をもつ，二重ガラス張り
のペントハウスがある．メトロポリタン・スクエアのルーフ・ラインの尖頂は，
夜間ドラマチックに照明を浴びてダウンタウンの夜空に注目を集め，この企業
のシンボルにまでなったニューヨーク市のメトロポリタン生命ビルの屋根の信
号灯「決してくじけない光」をも想起させる．

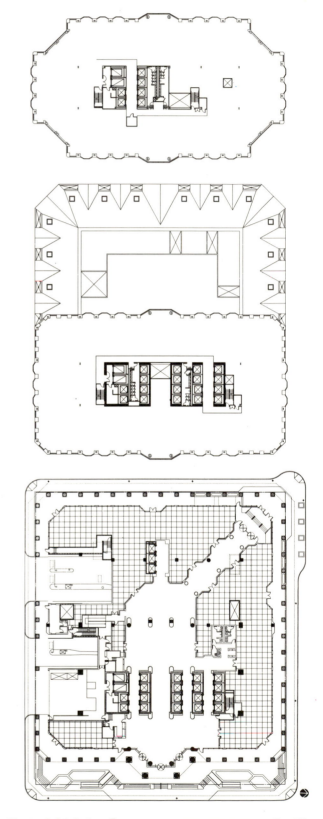

(top) Typical highrise floor
plan (32nd-39th).
(middle) Typical lowrise
floor plan (9th-15th).
(above) Ground floor plan.

（上）高層階基準階平面図（32階-39階）.
（中）低層階基準階平面図（9階-15階）.
（下）1階平面図.

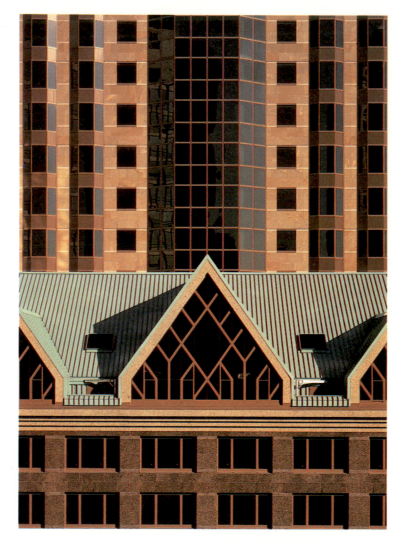

(p.143) *View of
Metropolitan Square, at
center, viewed from the
grounds of the Jefferson
Memorial Expansion Park.*
(pp.144-145) *Looking east
at the St. Louis skyline, with
Metropolitan Square at left,
the old Courthouse at right,
and the Gateway Arch and
the Mississippi River in the
background.*
(above) *Curtainwall and
dormer details of the
building's lower level, with
the tower rising in the
background.*

(p.147) *The tower viewed
from the west.*
Photos:
*p.143, pp.146-147, p.149
and p.151 by George Cott.
pp.144-145, p.148 and p.
150 by Robert Pettus.*

(p.143) ジェファーソン記念公園からみる.
(p.144-145) セントルイスのスカイライ
ン. 東方向を見る.
左にメトロポリタン・スクエア, 右手に
旧裁判所, 背後にサーリネンのアーチ,
ミシシッピ川が見える.
(上)カーテンウォールの外壁とドーマー
窓.
(p.147) 西側から見る.

FASHION GAL

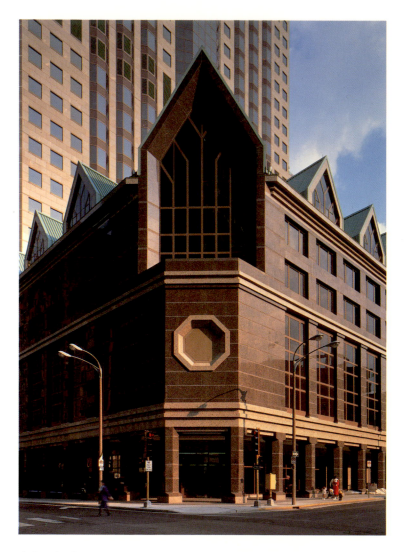

(*above*) *Sixth Street entrance.*
(*p.149*) *The pedestrian plaza outside the main entrance on the east side of the building.*

（上）６番街に面した入口.
(p.149) 東側の主玄関へのアプローチ.

(p.150) *Looking across the entry lobby to a mural by Terry Schoonhoven. The dome of the old Courthouse, shown in the mural, is also visible through the lobby's walls of Pilkington glass.*

(above) *The lobby, viewed from the east entrance. Between the elevator banks, a section of the Lincoln Perry mural is visible. Also note the marble-clad walls and coffered ceiling.*

(p.150) 正面にテリー・スクーンホーヴェンの壁画が見える．その壁画と外部に旧裁判所のドームが見える．
(上) 東側の主玄関からロビーを見る．奥にリンカーン・ペリーの壁画が見える．壁は大理石．

The Living World/St. Louis Zoo

St. Louis, Missouri, USA

セントルイス動物園リヴィング・ワールド
アメリカ，ミズーリ州セントルイス
1989

The Living World, a $17 million education center, celebrates the richness and diversity of the animal kingdom and the interrelatedness of all living things. It represents a major commitment by the St. Louis Zoo, one of the most prominent zoos in the world, to educate the public about vital issues relating to wildlife preservation and environmental conservation.

The 55,000-square-foot structure was designed to provoke curiosity and create an atmosphere of learning and enjoyment. The use of natural materials—brick, terra cotta, light-colored woods, stone, and glass, combined with the patinated copper—brings the building into harmony with its park setting. Organized with four two-story, octagonally-shaped wings clustered around a central, 60-foot-high skylit rotunda, the structure's faceted walls and roof break up its mass and lessen its scale.

Circulation is organized around the rotunda. On the upper level, two spacious educational exhibit halls, designed for use by adults and children, fuse state-of-the-art technology with the display of live animals. Within these halls, computer and video technology are mixed with living creatures in an information-dense, learning environment.

The Hall of Ecology contains a replica of a free-flowing Missouri Ozarks stream, along with interactive exhibits that emphasize the biological diversity found around the world. Visitors to the Hall of Animals are greeted by a robotic likeness of Charles Darwin, which introduces them to displays that illustrate wildlife's natural adaptations and the theory of evolution.

The two exhibit halls alone contain 85 three-minute films, 30 computer stations, 50 video screens, a dozen interactive video displays, and approximately 150 animals of various species. Also included on the top floor is a 400-seat auditorium, a stand-up theater for 100, and a public restaurant leading to an exterior deck with panoramic views of the Zoo.

The lower level of The Living World contains the offices of the Zoo's education department along with three modern classrooms outfitted with laboratory equipment, full audiovisual capabilities, and a "classroom of tomorrow," a computer-based interactive learning space linked to the rich visual and verbal data bases of the exhibits upstairs.

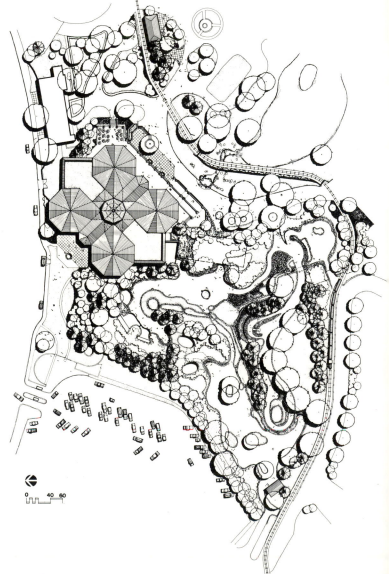

(right) Site plan.
(p.153) The Living World viewed from Forest Park.
(pp.154-155) The Living World vistor and education center, viewed from the grounds of the St. Louis Zoo.
Photos :
p.153, pp.154-155 and p.158 by George Cott.
Photos:
p.157 and pp.159-161 by Robert Pettus.

(右) 配置図.
(p.153) 森林公園から見た全景.
(p.154-155) セントルイス動物園から見たリヴィング・ワールド.

1,700万ドルをかけた教育センター，リヴィング・ワールドは，動物王国の豊かさと多様性を讃え，生きとし生けるものの相関性を理解しうる場所となっている．この施設は，世界で最も優れた動物園の一つに数えられるセントルイス動物園が主体となって，野生生物の保護と環境保全に関わる重要問題について社会一般に対して教育を試みるという施設である．

5万5,000平方フィートの建物は，好奇心を刺激し，楽しみながら学ぶ雰囲気をつくり出すように計画されている．材料には煉瓦やテラコッタ，明るい色の木材，石，ガラス，緑青のでた銅と組み合せたものなど，自然の素材を用い，建物と周辺の公園環境との調和を保っている．中央の高さ60フィートのスカイライトのあるロトンダを囲んで2階建ての八角形の棟が四つ配置され，切子面となった壁と屋根がこの建物全体を分割して，規模を小さく感じさせる．

展示動線システムはロトンダの周囲をめぐるように構成されている．上階には大人と子供がともに楽しむことのできる二つの広々とした展示ホールがあり，生きた動物の展示と最新のテクノロジーとが融合されている．これらの展示ホールでは，コンピュータとヴィデオの技術が生物たちと組み合されて，情報密度の濃い学習環境となっている．

エコロジー・ホールには，ミズーリ州のオザーク川の流れの模型が，世界で発見される生物学的多様性を示した関連展示とともに陳列されている．アニマル・ホールでは，チャールズ・ダーウィンを模したロボットが来館者を迎え，野生生物の自然への適合と進化論とを説明する展示に案内する．

この二つの展示ホールだけでも，85本の3分フィルムと30のコンピュータ・ステーション，50のヴィデオ・スクリーン，12の相互に関連したヴィデオ・ディスプレィ，様々な種の約150の動物などがある．さらに，上階には，400席の講堂と100名収容の立見劇場，動物園の全景を見晴らすことができる戸外のバルコニーにも出られるレストランなどがある．

リヴィング・ワールドの下階には動物園の教育課事務室の他に，実験設備を備えた三つの教室と視聴覚設備，さらに「未来教室」があり，ここは上階に展示された豊富な視覚的および言語的データ・ベースとつなげられたコンピュータによる相互学習の場となっている．

(*right top*) *Upper level plan.*
(*right bottom*) *Lower level plan.*
(*p.157*) *Detail of upper level showing atrium at twilight.*

（右上）上階平面図．
（右下）下階平面図．
（p.157）夕暮れ時のアトリウム上部．

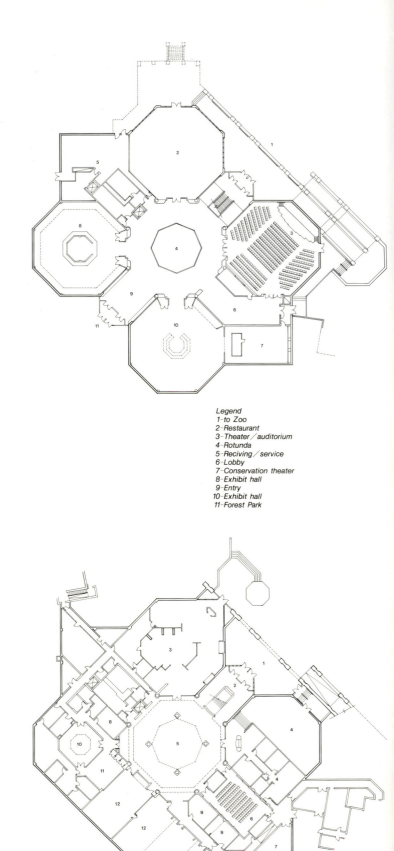

Legend
1-to Zoo
2-Restaurant
3-Theater／auditorium
4-Rotunda
5-Reciving／service
6-Lobby
7-Conservation theater
8-Exhibit hall
9-Entry
10-Exhibit hall
11-Forest Park

Legend
1-to Zoo
2-Entry
3-Gift shop
4-Education department office
5-Rotunda
6-Lecture hall
7-Animal room
8-Conference room
9-Work room
10-Board room
11-Zoo friends and Facility office
12-Class room

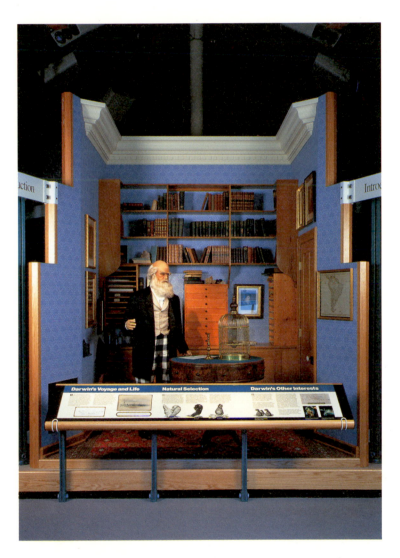

(p.158) *Visitors at The Living World.*
(*above*) *A life-size animated model of Naturalist Charles Darwin at entrance to the Hall of Animals.*

（p.158）２階アトリウム．展示室入口が見える．
（上）展示室入口のチャールズ・ダーウィンの等身大の人形によってアニマル・ホールに導かれる．

Senses

Spectrum and Vision

Bat Game

The Deep Oceans

Fish: The first vertebrates

Arthropods: The largest phylum

ER 40 TIMES THE LENGTH

Insects: The most numerous creatures

Crus

Uncommon Sense

Hunt Like a Bat

A closer look at the Senses

A Celebration of Insects

(*p.160*) *Squid sculpture hanging in the Hall of Animals.*
(*above*) *The Missouri Ozark Stream exhibit.*

（p.160）大きなイカが吊されている展示室アニマル・ホール.
（上）ミズーリのオザーク川の生態系の展示.

AmSouth/Harbert Plaza Mixed Use Center

with Gresham, Smith and Partners
Birmingham, Alabama, USA

アムサウス／ハーバート・プラザ多目的センター
アメリカ，アラバマ州バーミングハム
1989

The first phase of this major mixed-use project will include a
31-story office tower and a two-story, skylit retail atrium. A
distinctive addition to the Birmingham skyline, the tower rises to a
sculptured top capped by a copper-covered pyramid with corner
turrets crowned by globes.
The 702,000-square-foot office tower is clad in a golden Brazilian
granite, with windows of energy-efficient tinted glass. The landscaped
retail atrium, detailed with water features, contains 60,000 square
feet of retail space and also connects the tower with an adjacent
building, the AmSouth-Southern Natural Building. Four levels of
parking accommodate up to 400 cars below grade.
The center was developed as a joint venture between AmSouth Bank
and Harbert Corporation. A future phase of the project will include
a 250-room hotel or a 300,000-square-foot office building.

この大規模多目的プロジェクトの第1段階には，31階建て高層オフィス・タワ
ーとスカイライトのある2層吹抜けのショッピング・アトリウムが含まれる．
バーミングハムのスカイラインにひときわそびえるタワーの頂部は，四隅に球
体をいただく小塔のついた銅葺きのピラミッドがかぶせられている．
70万2,000平方フィートのオフィス・タワーは，金色のブラジル産花崗岩で覆わ
れ，窓にはエネルギー効率のよい色ガラスが使われている．造園の施されたシ
ョッピング・アトリウムは水を配して装飾され，60,000平方フィートのショッピ
ング・スペースをもち，また隣接するアムサウス・サザン・ナチュラル・ビル
とタワーとを結ぶ役割をしている．地下の4層の駐車施設には，400台までが駐
車できる．
このセンターはアムサウス銀行とハーバート社の合弁事業として計画された．
将来は250室のホテルや30万平方フィートのオフィス・ビルなども建設される予
定である．

(*right top*) West elevation.　　　（右上）西立面図．
(*right bottom*) Site plan.　　　　（右下）配置図．
(*p.163*) View from the　　　　　（p.163）通りからみる．
street.
Photos by George Cott.

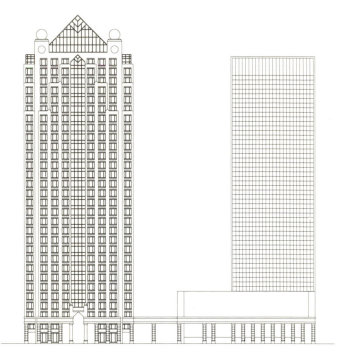

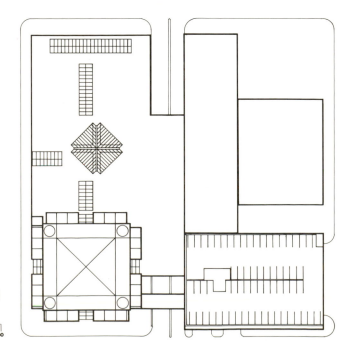

0   30

(*right top*) *3rd–16th floor plan.*
(*right middle*) *2nd floor plan.*
(*right bottom*) *Ground floor plan.*
(*p.165*) *View of the top of the AmSouth building.*

（右上）３−16階平面図.
（右中）２階平面図.
（右下）１階平面図.
（p.165）タワーの頂部を見る.

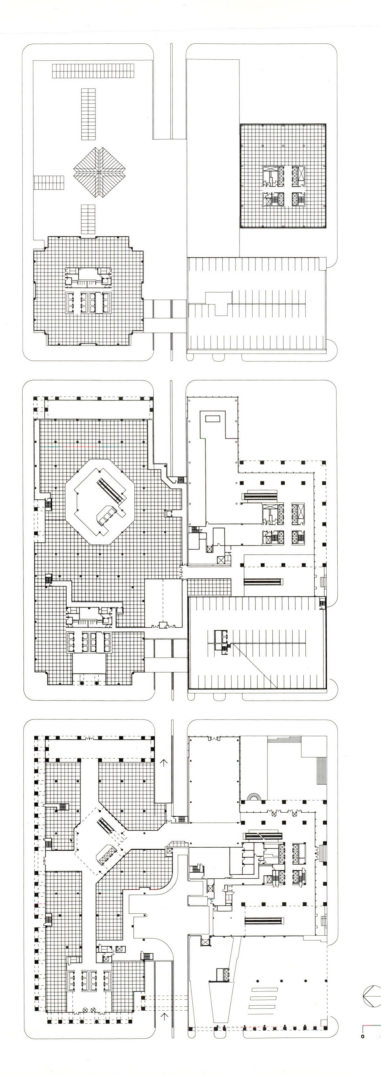

(p.166) The courtyard leading into the retail segment of the AmSouth building.
(above) Skylit food court area in the retail segment of the AmSouth building.

（p.166）アムサウス・ビルディングの店舗への入口となるコートヤード.
（上）店舗階のスカイライトのある喫茶室・レストラン.

801 Grand Avenue

with Brook, Borg & Skiles
Des Moines, Iowa, USA

801グランド・アヴェニュー・オフィス・タワー
アメリカ，アイオワ州デモイン
1990

At 44 stories, the 801 Grand Avenue commercial office development project will become the dominant building on the Des Moines skyline, symbolizing the economic vitality of the Quad Cities region. Each face of the skyscraper will be clad in golden Brazilian granite and punctuated with bronze-coated glass bays which lead to a peaked, eight-pointed star-shaped copper roof. Corner setbacks soften the impact of the building's mass while adding valuable corner office space to the floor plan.

The building's base features a marble-and-granite-clad, three-story atrium surrounded by commercial businesses. The third floor of the building is connected to Des Moines' skywalk system. A private business club will occupy the tower's top two floors, while parking for 90 cars will be located beneath the building. A large landscaped plaza helps integrate the building into the surrounding streetscape. Electrified floor decks throughout the structure will allow tenants to install flexible, custom-designed communications and computer systems.

44階建ての801グランド・アヴェニュー・ビルは，デモインのスカイラインにひときわ目立つビルとして，四連続都市地域の経済活力を象徴するものになろう．このスカイスクレイパーの各面は金色のブラジル産花崗岩で外装され，ブロンズ・ガラスのベイが八角の星形の銅葺き屋根の頂上までつづく．隅部のセットバックは，建物の威圧感を和らげる一方，平面計画上で隅部に貴重なオフィス・スペースを生み出している．

建物の基部は，様々な小売店に囲まれた3層吹抜けのアトリウムで，大理石と花崗岩の表面仕上げで特色をだしている．3階は，デモインのスカイ・ウォーク・システムに連結している．タワーの最上部2層には会員制ビジネス・クラブが入り，地下には90台収容の駐車場ができる予定である．造園の施された大きな広場が，周囲の街路の景観に建物を溶け込ませる役割を果たす．フロア・デッキには全館を通じて電気設備がなされており，テナントが独自にコミュニケーション設備やコンピュータ・システムを自由に設置できるようになっている．

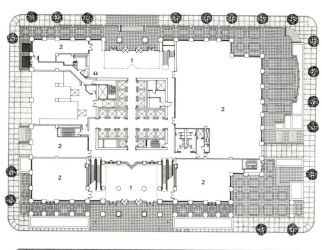

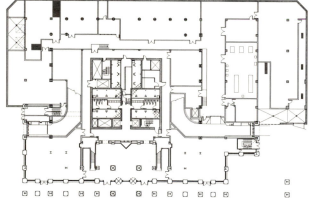

Legend
1-Lobby
2-Retail

(top right)Plan :site,level 1, level 2.
(bottom right) Ground level plan.
(p.169) Distant view from the east, shots early to mid morning.
Photos (pp.168-171) by Robert Pettus.

（右上）1,2階平面図．
（右下）地上階平面図．
（p.169）早朝，東側からの遠景．

(above) Entrance detail.
(p.171) View from the southeast.

（上）入口詳細.
(p.171) 南東側から見る.

Academic Research Building

J. Hillis Miller Health Center, University of Florida, Gainesville, Florida, USA

J・ヒリス・ミラー医療センター学術研究所
アメリカ，フロリダ州ゲインズヴィル，フロリダ大学
1990

With its curved entry facade, the Academic Research Building provides a distinct identity and a new "front door" for the J. Hillis Miller Health Center at the University of Florida in Gainesville. The Health Center contains the university's medical colleges, including the colleges of medicine, dentistry, nursing and pharmacy.
The six-story, 285,000-square-foot Academic Research Building is clad with architectural precast panels and brick. Horizontal brick banding, deep reveals and bullnose features add detail to the building's exterior skin, while precast sunshades over the windows create a playful pattern of light and shadow on the facade. The brick banding also creates a visual tie with the other Health Center buildings, which are mostly brick.
Curved rooftop parapets house mechanical equipment and echo the curves of the building's overall design. Individual exhaust stacks for laboratory fume hoods are grouped together in stainless steel housings, becoming a design element for the building.
The Academic Research Buidling is 80 percent laboratory space and 20 percent office/support space. The main office area, located above the entry, connects two laboratory wings which contain two double-loaded corridors with a common lab support area in between. Additional office/support areas are located at the opposite ends of the laboratory wings.
A two-story, open-air breezeway at the main entry provides access to the office and lab areas, as well as to a pedestrian concourse which runs the length of one lab wing. The concourse, which features a curved canopy of glass, connects the entry to the main circulation level of other buildings in the Health Center complex. The breezeway also allows pedestrians to pass directly through the Academic Research Building to reach other Health Center facilities clustered around an open courtyard with brick walkways that is located behind the building.

この学術研究所棟は，入口部分の外部構成が曲面を描いていて，これが際立った特徴となっており，ゲインズヴィルのフロリダ大学J・ヒリス・ミラー医療センターの新しい玄関口となっている．この医療センターには医科大学があり，医科，歯科，看護科，薬科の各専門大学がある．

6階建て28万5,000平方フィートのこの学術研究所棟は，外壁がプレキャスト・パネルと煉瓦であり，水平の煉瓦の帯，深い窓の窪み，端部が丸味を帯びた姿がこの建物の外観に深みを加えている．さらにプレキャストの日除けがファサードに光と影の戯れを生み出している．煉瓦の帯は，ほとんどが煉瓦の外壁となっている他の医療センターの建物との視覚的な結び付きをもたらしている．曲面を描く屋上パラペットはその内側に機械設備をもち，建物全体の曲線を帯びた形と呼応している．研究室個々の煙突はステンレス・スティールの排気筒の中にまとめられていて，この排気筒がこの建物のデザイン要素となっている．学術研究センターの80パーセントは研究室，20パーセントが事務室，維持施設となっている．主となる事務領域は入口上部にあり，二つの研究室棟を結んでいる．各研究室棟には二つの並走した通路があり，その間に研究室の維持施設が置かれている．研究室の端部には補助の事務室，維持施設がある．主玄関にある天井高が2階分の通り抜けの外部通路は，研究室棟の長さに沿う歩行者用のコンコースへと，さらに事務室，研究室への導入路となっている．このコンコースは曲面ガラスのキャノピーに覆われており，医療センターの他の施設の受付階への入口とつながっている．この外部通路によって，歩行者は学術研究所棟を通り抜け，この棟の背後の，煉瓦の遊歩道のある中庭の回りに配置された，医療センターの諸建物にゆくことができる．

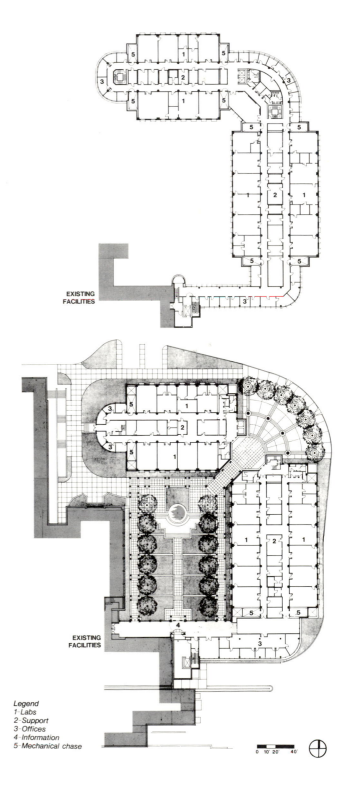

EXISTING FACILITIES

EXISTING FACILITIES

Legend
1-Labs
2-Support
3-Offices
4-Information
5-Mechanical chase

0 10' 20'   40'

(top) Typical-floor plan.
(above) First-floor plan.
(p.173) The curved entry facade viewed from the main campus.
Photos (pp.172-177) by George Cott.

（上）基準階平面図．
（下）1階平面図．
（p.173）メイン・キャンパスからカーヴを描いた入口ファーサードを見る．

(above) Detail of the curved
entry facade.
(p.175) A view across the
courtyard to the Academic
Research Building, taken from
the adjacent Medical Sciences
Building.

（上）カーヴを描いた入口ファサード詳
細.
（p.175）隣接する医療科学研究所脇から
中庭越しに学術研究所棟を見る.

(p.176) Courtyard steps lead to the concourse entry.
(above) The first floor concourse leads from the entry to the main circulation level of the Health Center complex.
The information desk, center right, is located opposite the courtyard entrance to the concourse.

(p.176)中庭を見る．階段が歩行者用コンコースへ導く．
（上）1階コンコースを見る．右手にインフォメーションが見える．反対側に中庭への出入口がある．

Columbia University Center for Engineering and Physical Science Research

New York, New York, USA

コロンビア大学工学自然科学研究センター
アメリカ，ニューヨーク州ニューヨーク
1991

Columbia University's Center for Engineering and Physical Science Research will provide state-of-the-art facilities for the university's expanding research programs in computer sciences, telecommunications, robotics, microelectronics and bioengineering. The six-story, 200,000-square-foot structure, located above a new, four-level, below-ground utility plant, contains laboratories, offices, research support facilities, an auditorium and a variety of seminar rooms and staff lounges. The laboratories are designed to accommodate future technological advancements of required electrical and communications systems.

The research center's design pays homage to the 19th-century planning and stylistic traditions of noted campus architects McKim, Mead and White, while projecting a high-tech image appropriate to its research activities.

Located at the northern terminus of the campus's central axis, the building's central block is deliberately monumental in design. Its roof style and precast concrete exterior recall the roof styles and limestone facades of other major buildings on the campus's central axis. Stone-like detailing of the concrete panels and punctured window openings further relate the structure to a series of older brick buildings, trimmed in limestone, that form the campus' outer perimeter. However, high-tech materials—such as metal window surrounds, transoms with ceramic patterned glass and high-capacity tube truss bridges—establish the research center's 21st-century orientation.

The research center is set back from the street to literally and symbolically open the northern end of the campus to the community. Gates originally designed for this purpose, but unused for years, are once again employed to create a major new entryway to the university.

この建物は，コンピュータ・サイエンスや電気通信学，ロボット工学，マイクロエレクトロニクス，生体工学などの各分野におけるする研究プログラムの拡大に対応し，最新の設備を提供するものである．

新しい4層の地下ユーティリティ施設の上に建てられる6階建て20万平方フィートの建物には，研究室と事務室，研究補助設備，講堂，各種セミナー・ルーム，スタッフ用ラウンジなどがつくられる．研究室は，必要とされる電気通信システムの将来における技術的な進歩に対応できるように設計されている．

この計画は，著名なキャンパス建築家のマッキム・ミード・ホワイトによる19世紀の計画や伝統様式に敬意を払いつつ，ここの研究活動にふさわしいハイ・テクのイメージを反映したものである．

このセンターがキャンパス中央軸の北端に位置するため，中央部は意図的に記念碑的な表現となっている．屋根の形とプレキャスト・コンクリートの外装は，キャンパス中央軸上の主な建物の屋根様式や石灰岩のファサードを想起させる．コンクリート・パネルの石積み様のディテールやくぼんだ小さな窓が，キャンパスの周辺の装飾石灰岩の煉瓦造の古い建物群との調和をはかっている．一方，金属の窓枠や陶質の装飾ガラスのトランサム，高性能鋼管トラスのブリッジなどのハイ・テク素材がセンターの21世紀への志向を表している．

このセンターは通りから引っ込んで建ち，キャンパス北端を地域社会に対して開いている．もともとはそういった目的で設計されていたゲートも，長く使われていなかったが，大学への新しい入口をつくりだすために再活用される．

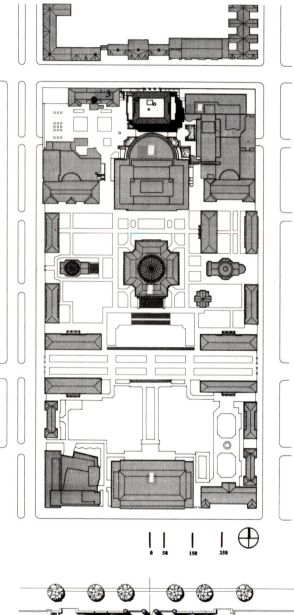

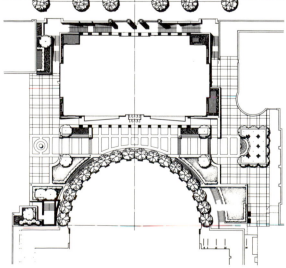

(p.178top) Site plan.
(p.178bottom) Detail of the
site plan.
(top) Rendering of the
southeast elevation, as viewed
from the campus.
(above) Detail of the south
elevation.

（P.178上）配置図.
（P.178下）配置図部分.
（上）キャンパス側の南東側から見たレン
ダリング.
（下）南面立面詳細.

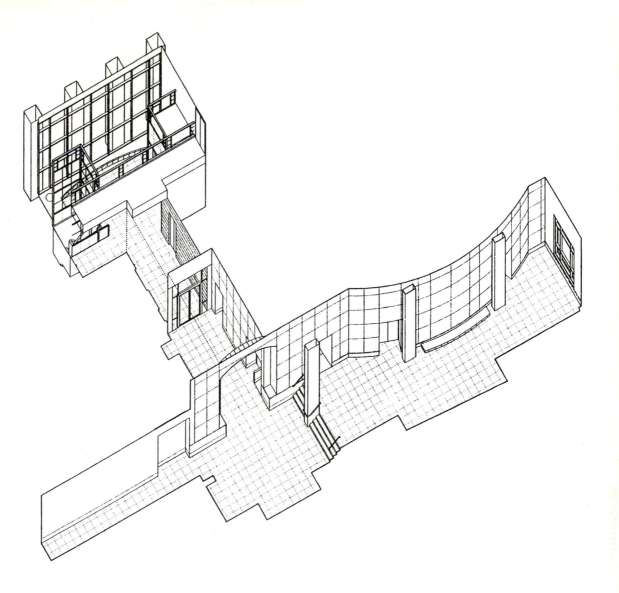

Legend
1-Laboratory
2-Service corridor
3-Research office
4-Administrative office

(p.180) Rendering of the northeast elevation, viewed from 120th street.
(top) Axonometric drawing of terrace level public spaces.
(above) Typical level plan.

（p.180）120番ストリート側の北東側から見たレンダリング.
（上）テラス階のアクソノメトリック・ドローイング.
（下）基準階平面図.

Wells Fargo Center at Capitol Mall

Sacramento, California, USA

キャピトル・モール・ウェルズ・ファーゴ・センター
アメリカ，カリフォルニア州サクラメント
1991

The Wells Fargo Center presents an accommodating design that reflects the needs of its occupants as well as its location in the state capitol of California.

Clad in a warm, rose-gray granite and a complementary precast concrete, the 30-story, 990,000-square-foot structure is set back from the street to maintain views of the state capitol building. A curved copper roof gives the building high visibility on the city's skyline, while a five-story atrium forms a grand entrance from the street. The atrium leads into an equally high lobby that will house a museum on the history of the "Gold Rush" era, which was critical to the state's development. Design elements recalling past architectural traditions—a barrell-vaulted, coffered ceiling; rich granite and marble cladding; and classical Renaissance floor patterns—will give the lobby a timeless quality.

The center will be home to the regional offices of the Wells Fargo Bank. It will also contain a restaurant and 500,000 square feet of leasable space. Tenant space on the 7th through 12th floors has been expanded slightly to offer larger-than-normal floor plates. Parking for 1,200 cars, integrated in the building's design with no visible manifestation at street level, will provide direct access to the building's lobby.

ウェルズ・ファーゴ・センターには，カリフォルニア州の州都に建つという条件とそこで働く人々の要求を反映するという設計意図が表れている．

暖かみのあるローズ・グレイの花崗岩に，補助的にプレキャスト・コンクリートを用いた外部仕上げの，30階建て99万平方フィートのこの建物は，州議事堂が見えるように，通りから引っ込んでいる．曲面を描く銅葺き屋根が町のスカイラインにくっきりと浮かび，通りからの入口は，5層吹抜けの大きなアトリウムになっている．このアトリウムから同じ高さのロビーへとつづくが，ロビーには，町の発展に大きな役割を果たした「ゴールド・ラッシュ」時代の歴史博物館がある．格間で飾った半円ヴォールトの天井，ふんだんに使った花崗岩と大理石，クラシックなルネサンス様式の床の模様など，こういった昔の建築の伝統を思わせるデザインが，このロビーに時代を超えた品格を与えている．

このセンターは，ウェルズ・ファーゴ銀行の各地域支店の本部となるものである．建物内には，レストラン一つと50万平方フィートのリース・スペースがさらに設けられる．7階から12階までのテナント・スペースは，通常より大きなプレート（敷桁）にするため少し広くしてある．1,200台収容の駐車場は，通りレヴェルから見えないように建物の中に統合され，ロビーに直接アクセスできるようになっている．

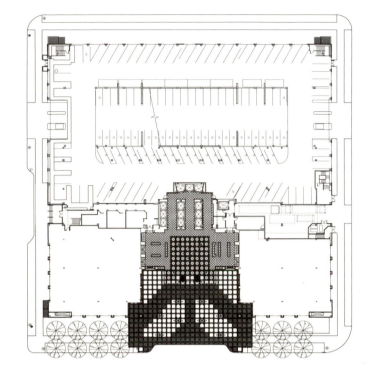

(*above*) *Site plan.*
(*p.183*) *Overall view of Wells Fargo Center* (*model*), *as it will look on the Sacramento, CA, skyline. Photos* (*pp. 182–185*) *by HOK Photography.*

（上）配置図．

（p.183）ウェルズ・ファーゴ・センターの模型をサクラメントの町にはめ込んだ完成予想モンタージュ．

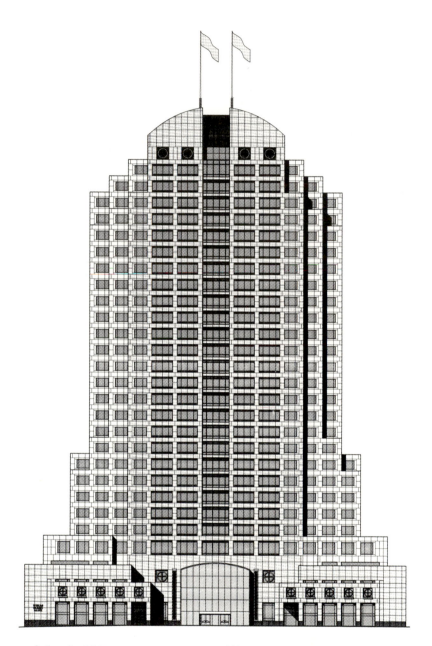

(*above*) *Main entrance elevation.*
(*p.185*) *Model of Wells Fargo Center lobby, with historic Wells Fargo coach on display.*

（上）メイン・エントランス側立面図.
（p.185）ウェルズ・ファーゴ・センターのロビー模型.歴史的に有名なウェルズ・ファーゴ駅馬車が展示されている.

Minami Office Tower

Las Vegas, Nevada, USA

ミナミ・オフィス・タワー
アメリカ，ネヴァダ州ラスヴェガス
1991

The Minami Office Tower planned for the city of Las Vegas will be, at 36 stories and 600,000 square feet, the tallest structure in the state of Nevada. Set apart from Las Vegas' entertainment district, the building's squared shape and peaked roof signal its businesslike atmosphere.

A 60-foot-high lobby connects several parking and retail levels, and places the first floor of offices high enough to provide panoramic daytime views of the mountains that surround this desert city and nighttime views of the brightly lit casinos along the Las Vegas strip. The upper office floors become smaller in size as the tower narrows in multiple setbacks towards its roof spire. These setbacks offer balcony terraces and a variety of floor sizes to prospective tenants. The top floor will be dedicated to restaurant facilities and observation space, so the tower will remain in use into the evening hours. The tower will be lit up at night to emphasize its role as an urban landmark.

ミナミ・オフィス・タワーは，ラスヴェガスに建設される36階建て60万平方フィートのビルで，ネヴァダ州で最も高い建物になる予定である．ラスヴェガスの歓楽街から離れて建ち，建物の四角い形と尖った屋根とが，実業的な雰囲気をもつ．

天井高60フィートのロビーは駐車場や各店舗フロアに連絡しており，オフィスの入る階は最下階でもかなりの高さにあって，日中はこの砂漠都市を囲む雄大な山並みを，夜間はラスヴェガス歓楽地帯の眩いカジノのきらめきを眺望できるほどである．

上層のオフィス・フロアは，タワーが屋根の尖塔に向かって段階的にセットバックして細くなるにつれ，面積が小さくなる．これらのセットバックによってテラスなどを確保でき，将来のテナントに対してフロア・サイズを多様に提供できる．最上階はレストランと展望台になる予定なので，タワーは夜間も使われることになる．都市のランドマークとしての役割を強調するため，タワーには夜間照明があてられる．

(*right*) Section.
(*p.187top left*) Twenty-third floor plan.
(*p.187top right*) Twenty-first floor plan.
(*p.187bottom left*) Third floor plan.
(*p.187bottom right*) Ground floor plan.
Photos (*pp.186–189*) by HOK Photography.

(右) 断面図．
(p.187左上) 23階平面図．
(p.187右上) 21階平面図．
(p.187左下) 3階平面図．
(p.187右下) 1階平面図．

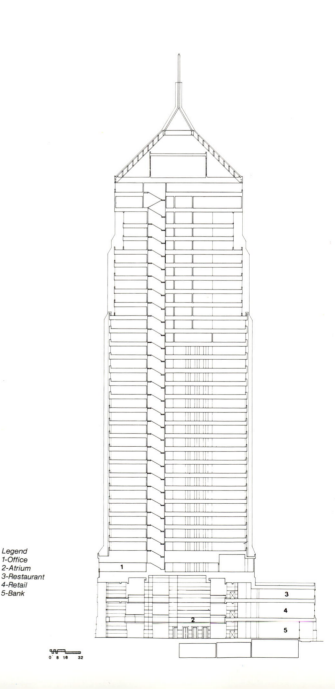

Legend
1-Office
2-Atrium
3-Restaurant
4-Retail
5-Bank

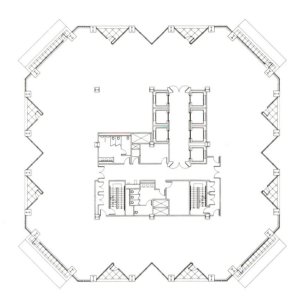

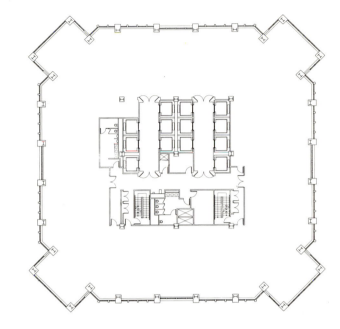

Legend
1-Restaurant
2-Retail
3-Lobby below
4-Drive-up teller

5-Bank lease area
6-Receiving
7-Security
8-Atrium
9-Valet

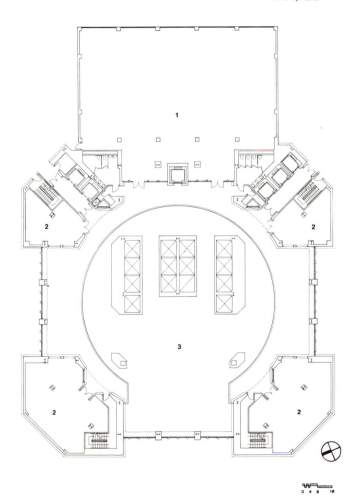

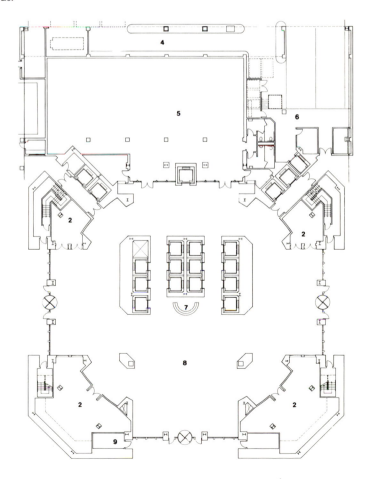

0 4 8 16

(*above*) *Detail showing top of Minami Tower* (*model*). (*p.189*) *Rendering of Minami Tower, as view from the west.*

（上）模型頂部詳細.
(p.189) 西側から見たレンダリング.

Camden Yards Twin-Stadium Complex

Baltimore, Maryland, USA

カムデン・ヤーズ・ツイン・スタジアム
アメリカ，メリーランド州ボルチモア
1992

Camden Yards Twin-Stadium Complex, a 46,000-seat baseball park, will be home to the Baltimore Orioles when it is completed in 1992. Designed as an "old-time" ballpark, Camden Yards will fit into its historic neighborhood while providing modern amenities to the city's baseball fans. A 65,000-seat football stadium is planned for a later phase of the project.

カムデン・ヤーズ・ツイン・スタジアムは，4万6,000席のベースボール・スタジアムで，1992年の完成後はボルチモア・オリオールズのホーム・グラウンドになる予定である。「昔風の」野球場に設計されたカムデン・ヤーズは，周囲の古い建物と調和し，かつボルチモアの野球ファンに現代的なアメニティ施設をもたらすものである。また，このプロジェクトの後には，6万5,000席のフットボール・スタジアムも計画されている。

(p.190) *View toward the home plate entry.*
(top) *Site plan.*
(above) *View toward the score board. The old warehouse is visible at right of the background.*

（p.190）ホーム・プレート側入口に向かって見る.
（上）配置図.
（下）バック・スクリーンに向かって見る. 背後右手に古い倉庫が見える.

Cervantes Convention Center Expansion & Domed Stadium

with Kennedy Associates/Architects, Inc. (expansion)
St. Louis, Missouri, USA

セルヴァンテス・コンヴェンション・センター増築およびドーム・スタジアム
アメリカ，ミズーリ州セントルイス
1993

The Cervantes Convention Center in St. Louis, designed by HOK in the mid-1970s, is being expanded from 471,000 to 941,000 square feet. Additionally, a new 1,711,000-square-foot domed stadium, also designed by HOK, will be built on the east side of the convention complex. Together, these additions will provide 500,000 square feet of exhibit floor space, making Cervantes the second-largest, continuous single-floor exhibit space in the United States. This will allow the city to attract substantially larger conventions, exhibitions and trade shows, as well as major entertainment and sporting events. The Cervantes expansion will create a new entrance on the south side of the convention center, facing the downtown central business district. The center's south facade will feature a crescent-shaped pedestrian plaza that is recessed from the street, and a 110-foot-tall rotunda that will be illuminated at night. A tower at the southeast corner of the facility will house the St. Louis Visitors Center.
At the juncture of the convention center and the stadium, a Picadilly Circus-like commons area will link the facilities and provide access to a new auditorium/lecture hall. It will also serve as the north/south circulation spine for convention-goers and downtown pedestrians, and lead to the proposed site of a new convention center hotel.
The new multi-purpose domed stadium will be able to seat up to 70,000 people for a sporting or entertainment event, or up to 22,800 people on one level for a convention. It will have retractable seats which can be folded into the walls to provide 160,000 square feet of exhibit floor space. Its truss-supported fabric roof and movable lighting grid can also be adjusted to better accommodate trade shows and exhibitions.

このコンヴェンション・センターは，1970年代の中頃 HOK によって設計されたものだが，これまでの47万1,000平方フィートから94万1,000平方フィートに増築され，さらに HOK によって，171万1,000平方フィートのドーム・スタジアムもこのコンヴェンション・センターの東側に建設される．この増築でセルヴァンテスは50万平方フィートの展示面積を有することになり，ひとつづきの展示面積としては，全米で第2の広さとなる．これが完成すれば，演劇や音楽そしてスポーツなどのイヴェントはもちろん，大展示会や貿易見本市を，セントルイスに呼ぶことができるだろう．

この増築は，ダウンタウンのビジネス地区に面しているセルヴァンテスの南面に，新しい玄関口をつくりだす．この南側のファサードでは，通りから引っ込んだ三日月形のペデストリアン・プラザと，夜に光り輝く，高さ110フィートのロトンダが特長をなす．東南の角にあるタワーにはセントルイス観光センターが入る予定である．

コンヴェンション・センターとスタジアムの間にはピカデリー・サーカスのような共用領域がある．ここはオーディトリアムや講堂への導入部ともなり，さらにセルヴァンテスにくる人やダウンタウンを歩く人のために南北方向の通り抜けの役割を果たし，計画されているホテルにも導く．

多目的のドーム・スタジアムは，スポーツや演劇・音楽ショウなどのために7万席まで収容でき，各種の大会や集会には，1フロアで2万2,800席を設けられる．また16万平方フィートの展示空間をつくりだせるように，壁の中にたたみ込まれる格納席が設けられ，トラスの屋根と可動の照明グリッドによって，貿易見本市や展示会にもうまく対応できるように考慮されている．

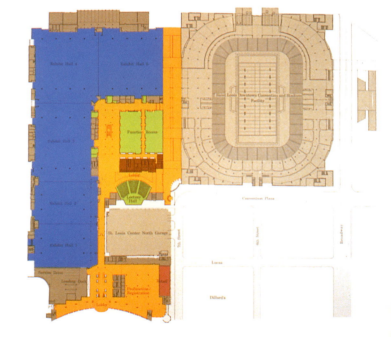

(above) Ground level plan of the Cervantes Convention Center and domed stadium. (The existing convention center facilities are shown in blue ; the addition is shown in yellow and green.)
Photo (p.193 bottom) by Brian Kuhlmann.

（上）ドーム形のスタジアムとセルヴァンテス・コンヴェンション・センターの1階平面図．（既存部分は青で，今回の増築部分は黄色と緑で示す．）

(top) A rendering of the proposed domed stadium, which will be connected to the east side of the Cervantes Convention Center and provide additional space for sporting and entertainment events as well as trade shows and conventions.
(above) Model shot of the new south entrance.
(pp.194-195) Rendering of the new south entrance to the Cervantes Convention Center in St. Louis.

（上）ドーム・スタジアムのレンダリング．スタジアムはセルヴァンテス・コンヴェンション・センターの東側に連結され，展示会や会議だけでなくスポーツやその他の各種催し物を行うことのできるスペースを提供することになる．
（下）新設された南側入口．
(p.194-195)新設された南側入口側からのレンダリング．湾曲したファサードが見える．

The Temple: Reorganized Church of Jesus Christ of Latter Day Saints

Independence, Missouri, USA

ザ・テンプル：末日聖徒イエス・キリスト改革教会世界本部
アメリカ，ミズーリ州インディペンデンス
1993

Conceived as the centerpiece of the world headquarters of the Reorganized Church of Jesus Christ of Latter Day Saints (RLDS), the Temple's design takes its inspiration from the spiral form of the chambered nautilus. The spiral, a timeless form that is associated worldwide with life, energy and growth, seemed an appropriate symbol for the RLDS Church. And, since a spiral can be viewed as shape that radiates outward or one that gathers and unifies inward to a central point, the design also relates to the church's concept of the Temple site as "the Center Place" from which the kingdom of God on earth will originate.

Over 200 feet wide at its base, the temple forms a spire rising 300 feet high. A glazed clerestory of clear glass follows the spiral of the sloped roof, allowing natural light to filter into the 2,000-seat sanctuary chamber. The Temple will be clad in Isola stone, a nearly pure white, smooth-finish stone that, along with the stainless steel roof, will glisten in the sunlight.

The Worshippers' Path, a long hallway that follows the Temple's curve, will lead members of the congregation and visitors from the skylit reception area to the main sanctuary. All along the hallway, wall niches containing religious artwork will encourage reflection and contemplation. Inside the sanctuary, vaulted drywall ceilings will arc upward over semi-circular rows of wood pews facing the centrum.

The Church's school and administrative facilities are located in an L-shaped wing that extends to the south and east of the Temple. Connected to the Temple by the two-story reception hall, the administrative wing will be clad in a light-colored, split-faced stone. This wing will contain a theater and lecture halls with fixed seating, as well as classrooms and offices.

A grand public plaza, natural meadow area and sculpture garden will complete the design for the 13-acre Temple site, which will also include parking for 700 vehicles.

末日聖徒イエス・キリスト改革教会の世界本部とされるザ・テンプルの計画は，オウム貝の螺旋形からヒントを得ている．生命，エネルギー，成長などになぞらえられる永遠の時代を超えた形態である螺旋形は，この計画にふさわしいシンボルと思われる．さらに，螺旋形は外に向かって広がる，あるいは中心点に向かって集まり一つになっているとも見えるため，教会堂は地上における神の国の原点となる「中心地」であるという，教会の概念にもかなっている．

ザ・テンプルは幅200フィートを超える基壇上に高さ300フィートの尖塔がそびえ，透明ガラスの高窓が，螺旋形の傾斜屋根に沿っており，2,000席の聖堂に自然光が差し込むようになっている．純白に近いなめらかな仕上げのアイソラ石で被覆され，ステンレスの屋根とともに陽光にきらめくだろう．

ザ・テンプルの曲面に沿った長い回廊，「礼拝路」は，教会の信徒や訪問客を，自然光の差し込むレセプション・エリアから内陣に導く．廊下に沿った壁龕には宗教的芸術作品が飾られ，内省と黙想とを促す．聖堂内部は半円弧状に列を成す木製の会衆席の上に，円形の乾式工法の天井が上方に向かって弧を描く．

教会の学校と本部施設は，南と東に伸びるL字形の建物に配されている．2層吹抜けのレセプション・ホールによってザ・テンプルとつながる本部棟は，明るい色の小割り石で被覆される．この棟には，教室と事務室の他に劇場と固定席をもつ講堂がある．

この5ヘクタールの敷地の計画は，広い公共広場や自然の草地，彫刻庭園，700台収容の駐車場などが決定すれば完了となる．

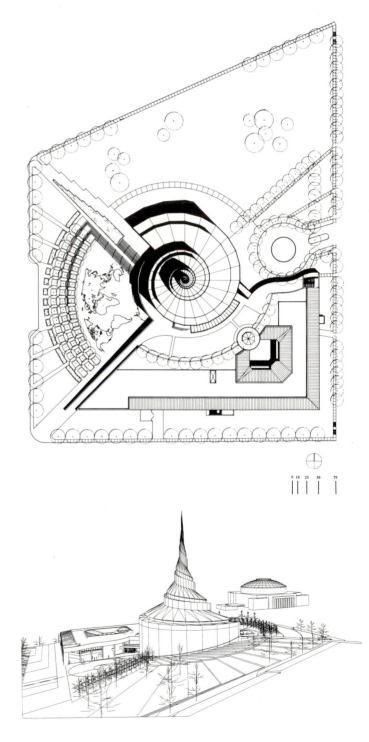

(top) Site plan.
(above) Perspective view by computer drawing.

（上）配置図.
（下）コンピュータ・ドローイングによる透視図.

(left top) Upper level plan.
(left bottom) Lower level plan.

（左上）上階平面図.
（左下）下階平面図.

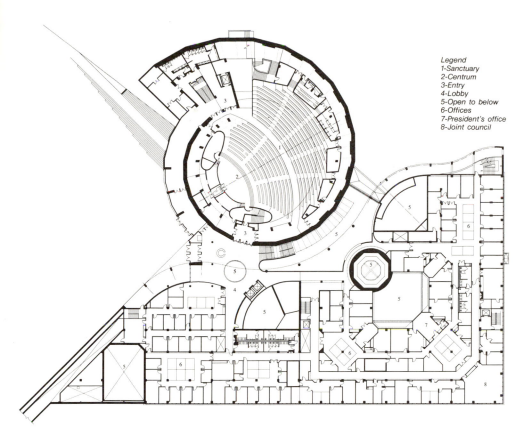

Legend
1-Sanctuary
2-Centrum
3-Entry
4-Lobby
5-Open to below
6-Offices
7-President's office
8-Joint council

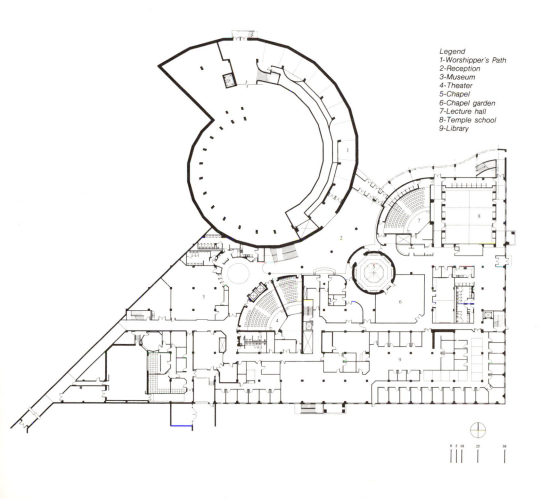

Legend
1-Worshipper's Path
2-Reception
3-Museum
4-Theater
5-Chapel
6-Chapel garden
7-Lecture hall
8-Temple school
9-Library

(above) General view
(p.199) Section perspective by
computer drawing.

（上）全景.
（p.199）コンピュータ・ドローイングによる
断面パース.

Kings County Hospital Center

Brooklyn, New York, USA

キングス・カウンティ・ホスピタル・センター
アメリカ，ニューヨーク州ブルックリン
1997

Kings County Hospital Center is a major teaching hospital and civic institution in New York City. To meet the changing needs of patients and to facilitate the adoption of new technologies and new modes of health care delivery, the New York City Health and Hospitals Corporation has commissioned HOK in association with Ellerbe Becket to design a major new health care facility.

The project consists of the 1,256-bed main hospital, a new 320-bed long-term-care facility, an ambulatory care building, a food services building, and the renovation of existing buildings.

The new facility is organized into two major groupings of nursing units. The main tower rises above a four-story base of support services, treatment, emergency and surgical areas. The second tower contains psychiatric nursing units and a prison hospital.

The base of the main hospital will be clad in precast masonry panels while the nursing units will be sheathed in rose colored brick which will relate in color and texture to the existing buildings.

キングス・カウンティ・ホスピタル・センターは，ニューヨークの中心的な教育研究病院であり，市民の医療機関でもある．患者の要求の変化に対応し，新しい技術や新しい健康管理・デリヴァリー方式の採用を容易にするため，ニューヨーク・シティ・ヘルス・アンド・ホスピタルズ・コーポレーションが，新しい大規模な健康管理施設の設計を，エレブ・ベケットとともに HOK に委託したものである．

このプロジェクトに含まれるものは，1,256床の主病棟と新しい320床の長期介護施設，巡回介護施設，給食サーヴィス施設，現在の建物の改築などである．新規に建築される施設は，二つの看護棟に大別して構成される．メイン・タワーは，補助サーヴィス，治療施設，救急外科分野などの入る4階建ての基部から立ちあがるように建てられる．もう一つのタワーには，精神科看護棟と刑務所病院ができる．

主病棟の土台部分はプレキャストの石積みパネルによって被覆され，一方，看護棟はばら色の煉瓦による被覆で，現存の建物の色や感触になじむものとなろう．

(right top) South elevation.
(right middle) Nursing unit.
(right bottom)First level plan:
west part.

（右上）南立面図．
（右中）看護病棟ユニット．
（右下）1階平面図（西部分）．

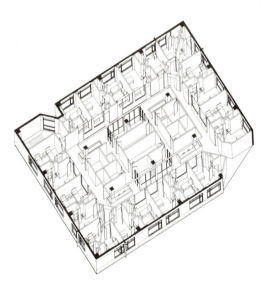

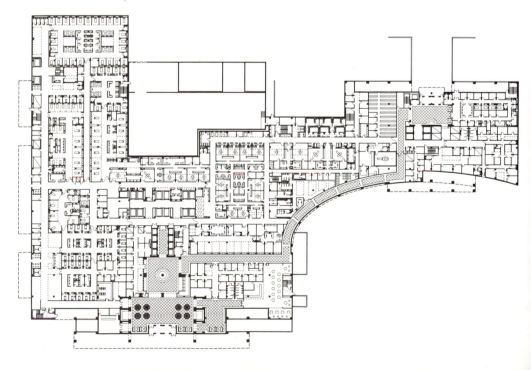

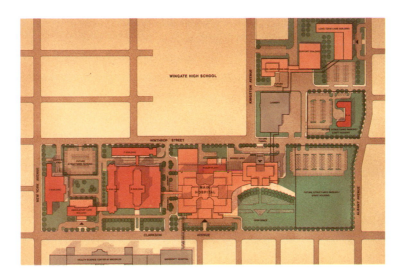

(top) Main hospital master
plan.
(above) New hospital main
tower from the southeast by
computer drawing.
(pp.202–203) Rendering of
exterior view.

（上）主病院マスター・プラン.
（下）コンピュータ・ドローイングによる
新病棟タワー. 東南から見る.
（p.202-203）全景. 左手の主病棟は，4つ
の看護病棟で構成されている.

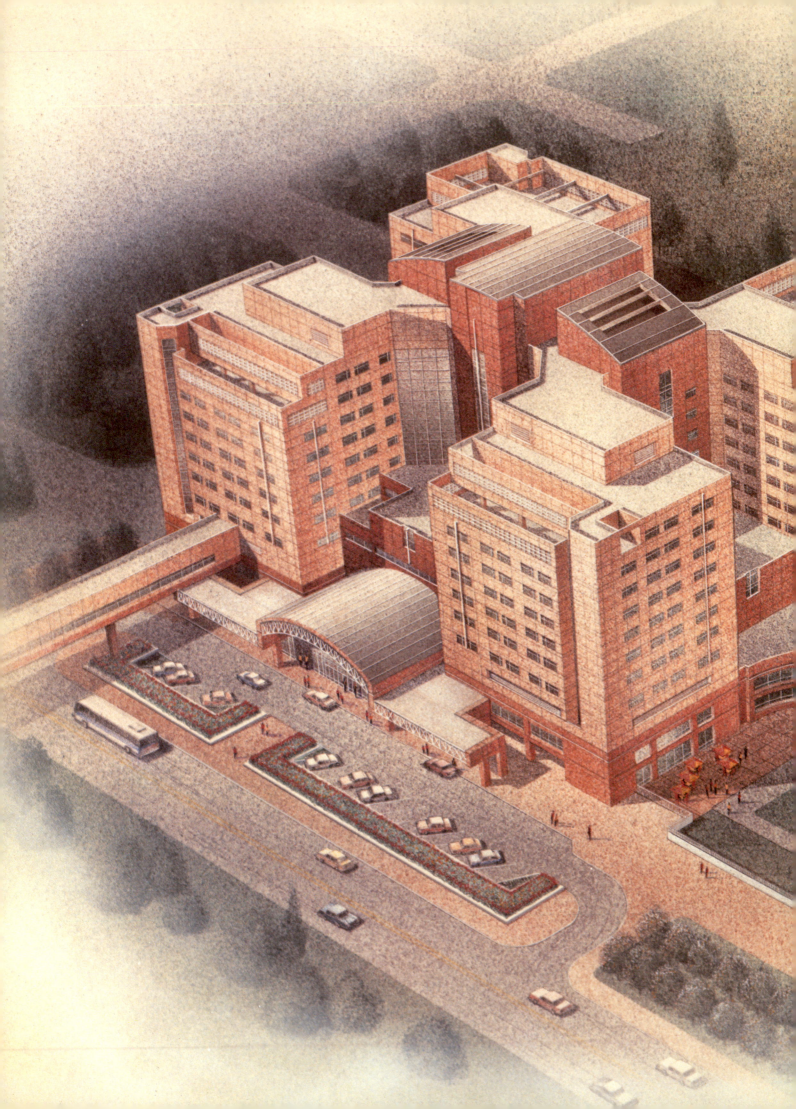

Brickell Gateway

Miami, Florida, USA

ブリッケル・ゲートウェイ
アメリカ，フロリダ州マイアミ
(future)

Rising 51 stories above Miami's financial district, the Brickell Gateway office tower will create a new landmark on the Miami skyline. Other components of the mixed-use complex include three levels of retail, a major hotel and 100 condominium units.
The hotel tower and condominiums will offer magnificent views of Miami and Biscayne Bay. The Gateway towers—with their overscaled domes, arches, setbacks, plazas, and natural stone cladding—will project a classic but contemporary profile while recalling the Mediterranean style that influenced Miami's early 20th century architecture during its golden era.
An urban plaza, surrounded by cafes and designed for outdoor entertainment, will lead to the 300,000-square-foot retail mall. A three-story, glass-enclosed entry and rooftop skylights will add drama to the space.
Brickell Gateway will provide office tenants with an array of services, including meeting and conference facilities, daycare facilities, catering services, health and exercise facilities, a full-service business center, and a private business club. Condominium tenants will be able to share amenities with hotel guests, including a spa, pool, jogging and tennis facilities, and a rooftop garden.
Nine levels of parking will serve the Brickell Gateway complex, connecting all facilities.

マイアミの金融街にそびえる51階建てのオフィス・タワー，ブリッケル・ゲートウェイは，マイアミのスカイラインを彩る新しいランドマークとなるだろう．この多目的利用のコンプレックスは三層のショッピング・スペース，大きなホテル，および100ユニットのコンドミニアムを擁している．
ホテル・タワーとコンドミニアムからは，マイアミとビスケーン湾の雄大な景色を見渡せる．特大のドームやアーチ，セットバック，広場，自然石を使った表面被覆など，ゲートウェイ・タワー群は，古典的にして現代的なプロフィールを表すものとなる．それは20世紀初期の黄金期のマイアミ建築に影響を与えた地中海様式を彷彿とさせよう．
戸外での催しのために設計されたアーバン・プラザは，カフェに囲まれた30万平方フィートのショッピング・モールにつづく．3層吹抜けのガラス張りの入口とスカイライトからの光が空間に劇的な雰囲気を添える．
ブリッケル・ゲートウェイは，テナントのオフィスに対し，会議施設や託児施設，ケータリング・サーヴィス，スポーツ保健施設，フルサーヴィスのビジネス・センター，会員制ビジネス・クラブなど，包括的なサーヴィス体制を整える予定である．コンドミニアムの入居者は，温泉やプール，ジョギング，テニスなどの施設，屋上ガーデンなどをホテルの宿泊客と共有できることになる．
このコンプレックス内には9層の駐車場が設けられ，全施設に連絡する．

(right top) West elevation.　　(右上）西立面図．
(right) Site plan.　　　　　　（右下）配置図．

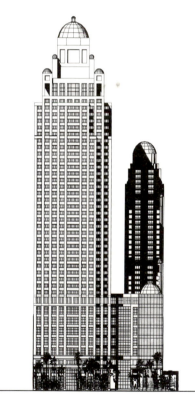

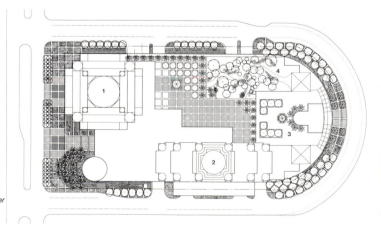

Legend
1-Office tower
2-Residential tower
3-Cabana level
4-Sky garden

0　25　50　　100

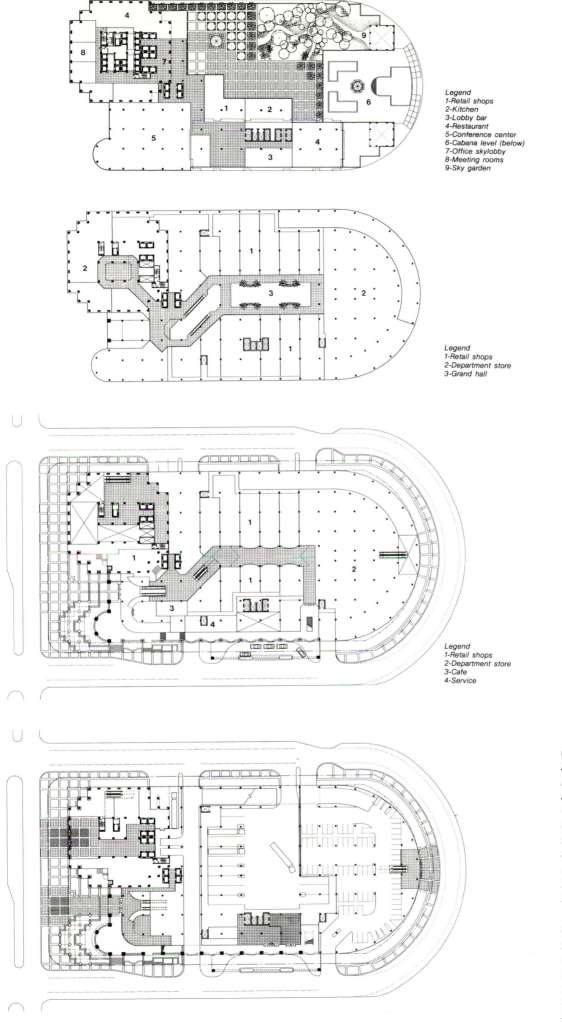

Legend
1-Retail shops
2-Kitchen
3-Lobby bar
4-Restaurant
5-Conference center
6-Cabana level (below)
7-Office skylobby
8-Meeting rooms
9-Sky garden

Legend
1-Retail shops
2-Department store
3-Grand hall

Legend
1-Retail shops
2-Department store
3-Cafe
4-Service

(left:from top to bottom)
Sky lobby floor plan.
Fourth floor plan.
Second floor plan.
Ground floor plan.
(pp.206-207) Rendering of
the Brickell Gateway complex
dropped into a photograph of
its Biscayne Bay site.
Photo (pp.206-207) by HOK
Photography.

(左：上から下に)
スカイ・ロビー平面図.
4階平面図.
2階平面図.
1階平面図.
(p.206-207) ビスケーン湾とブリッケル・
ゲートウェイ. 空中撮影写真にレンダリ
ングをはめこんだもの.

0 25 50   100

Retirement Park at Tokushima Prefecture

Tokushima, Japan

徳島県高齢者村マスター・プラン
徳島県

(Master plan in 1988)

The 129.5 hectare (320 acre) coastal retirement park at Tokushima Prefecture is designed to accommodate a growing elderly population by providing recreational, cultural and health care services in an integrated retirement community.

The heart of the design strategy for the community is one of its main recreational facilities, an 18-hole golf course. All residential units—including more than 1,500 independent-living villas, and congregate and garden-view apartments—overlook the green which extends the length of the site.

A town center surrounding a circular marina is the project's other dominant organizing element. Completing the list of major components are a health-care facility with services tailored to an aging population, and assisted and long-term care facilities.

To encourage residents to continue to live active, independent lives, the park provides an array of facilities and services, from performing arts and education centers to a health club, a two-level shopping mall, adult and child daycare, and a guest hotel. The park's recreational and cultural facilities are designed to attract non-residents to the public areas of the park, thereby providing residents with opportunities for meaningful social interaction with people from a variety of age groups.

徳島県の海岸沿いの129.5ヘクタールの高齢者村は，増えつつある高齢者のために保養，文化，厚生などのサーヴィスを統合した場で提供するという目的で設計されている．

この高齢者村の計画構想の中心は，その主要レクリエーション施設のひとつとなっている18ホールのゴルフ場である．1,500戸の1戸建てヴィラや庭付き集合住宅などのすべての住居からは，敷地一面に広がる緑が見渡せる．

円形のマリーナを囲むタウン・センターも，このプロジェクトのもう一つの重要な構成要素である．さらに，他のおもな施設をあげれば，高齢者に合せたサーヴィスを行う医療施設や介添者付きの長期介護施設などがある．

居住者が積極的な自立した生活をつづけられるように，この村では，芸能や学習センター，ヘルス・クラブ，2階建てのショッピング・モール，成人用デイケア施設，託児所，来客用ホテルなどの施設とサーヴィス機能を整えている．村のレクリエーション施設や文化施設は，居住者以外の人々をも村の公共領域にひきつけるように計画され，居住者があらゆる年齢層の人々との有意義な交流の機会をもちうるように考えられている．

(right) Overall master plan of the Retirement Park at the Tokushima Prefecture.
(p.209) Detail of the marina, which is encircled by retail shops, apartments, a cultural center and other facilities.
Photos by HOK Photography.

（右）マスター・プラン．
（p.209）マリーナ．周囲には店舗，集合住宅，文化センターなどの施設がある．

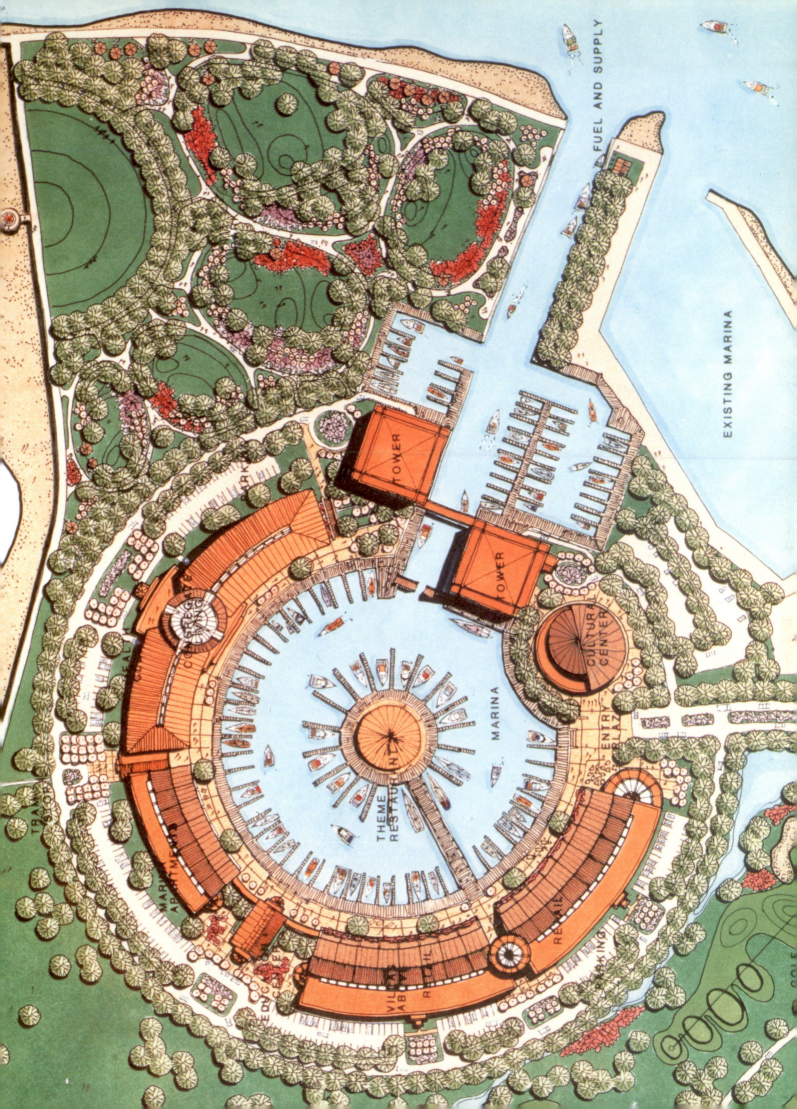

FUEL AND SUPPLY

EXISTING MARINA

TOWER

TOWER

MARINA

THEME RESTAURANT

CULTURAL CENTER

ENTRY PLAZA

RETAIL

PARKING

VILLAGE CABINS

RETAIL

EDGE CAFE

MARINA APARTMENTS

TRANS SHOPS

New York Hospital

with Taylor Clark Architects, Inc.
New York, New York, USA

ニューヨーク・ホスピタル
アメリカ，ニューヨーク州ニューヨーク

(future)

New York Hospital, one of the city's most respected health care institutions, has embarked upon a major capital improvement program to expand, upgrade and update its facilities, most of which were built in the 1930s. HOK has been commissioned by the hospital to conduct a facility assessment study and to make design recommendations.

As part of the study, HOK has explored a variety of site and building configuration options to determine which would best match the hospital's operational needs and priorities as well as its budget requirements. It is likely that 400-500 beds will be added in the first phase of the expansion program. The hospital currently has 1,000 beds. Overall, the project will likely encompass 700,000 to 1,000,000 square feet of renovation and new construction.

Because of site limitations, two design options under consideration at the time of this writing (Fall 1989) include the addition of several stories to existing hospital wings, or the creation of a new wing that would extend over FDR Drive on the east side of the hospital site. The hospital has an option on the air rights over the highway.

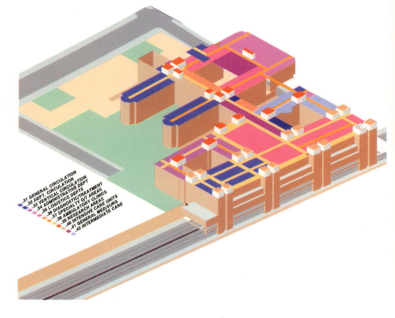

この病院は，ニューヨーク市で最も信頼のある医療機関の一つであるが，その大半が1930年代に建てられた施設を拡張し，グレード・アップし，近代化するという一大改善プログラムに着手している．HOK は病院側から施設の評価と設計についての推薦プラン作成を委託された．

HOK は，調査の一環として，病院の予算条件とともに運営上の要求と優先事項に最適の様々な配置と建築形態を検討した．第一次の拡張計画では，400〜500床が増設される見通しである．現在のベッド数は1,000床であるが，プロジェクト全体の改築および新築の面積は70〜100万平方フィートに及ぶだろう．

敷地の制約上，1989年秋の時点で検討中の二つの計画例は，現病棟に数階をのせるか，あるいは病院敷地の東側の FDR 自動車道の上に伸びるような形で新しい増築棟を建設するかのいずれかとなっている．病院は，このハイウェイ上の地上権をもっている．

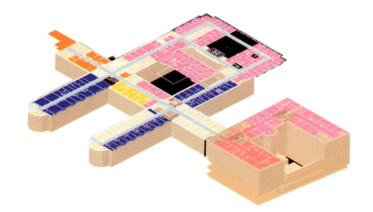

(top) Cut-away aerial perspective showing existing and proposed new building, with color-coded areas.
(bottom) Cut-away aerial perspective of existing facilities at 3rd floor level, with color-coded areas of proposed renovation.
(p.211) Perspective view of the proposed expansion of New York Hospital, including a facade study. (As viewed from Roosevelt Island).
(pp.212-213) Aerial perspective showing existing building massing superimposed with exploded view of proposed plans.
Photos (pp.210-213) by Jack Ward Color Service, Inc.

（上）既存棟と増築棟を示すパースペクティヴ．
（下）3 階の既存施設と改築部分を示すパースペクティヴ．
（p.211）ルーズヴェルト島から見た増築部分のパースペクティヴ．ファサード・スタディを含む．
（p.212-213）既存棟と増築棟のプランを合成したパースペクティヴ．

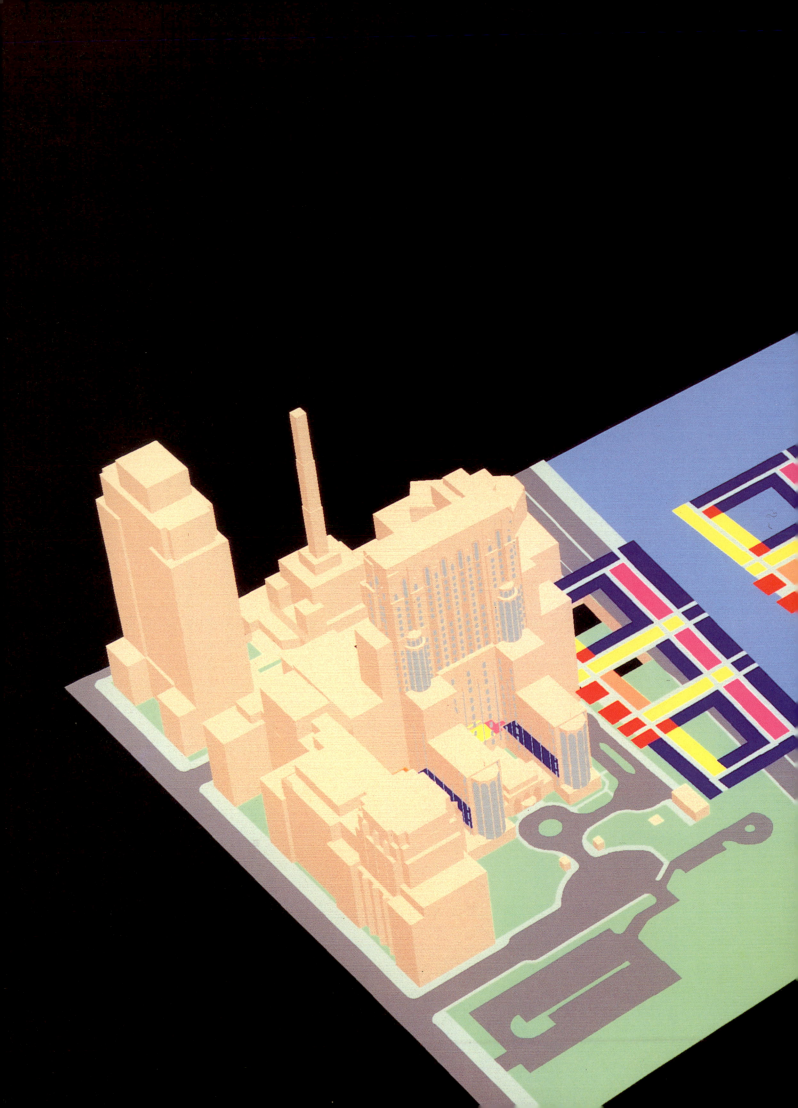

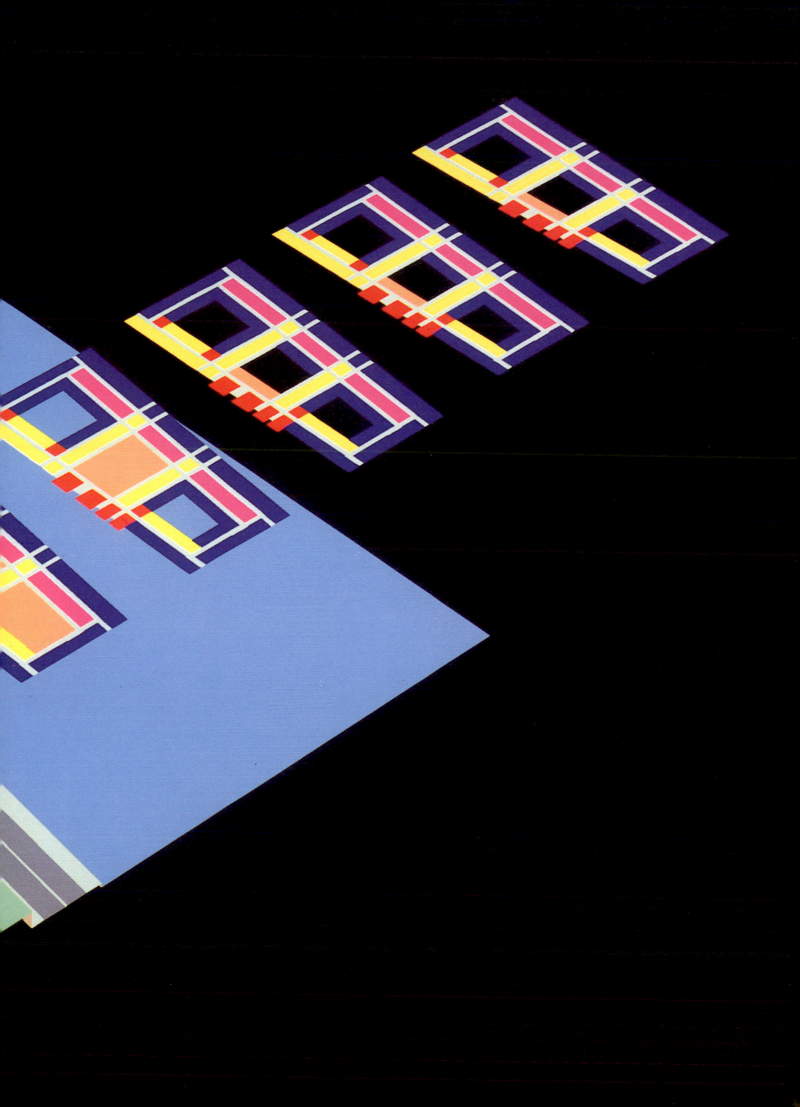

Northwest Airlines World Travel Center

with McClier Avitation Group, Greiner Engineering, and Nathan Johnson & Associates, Inc.
Wayne County Airport, Detroit, Michigan, USA

ノースウェスト航空ワールド・トラヴェル・センター
アメリカ，ミシガン州デトロイト，ウェイン郡空港
(Design Competition in 1990)

HOK was invited to submit a design for a new passenger terminal for Northwest Airlines at Wayne County Airport in Detroit, Michigan. The new terminal is intended to strengthen Northwest Airlines' and British Airways' positions as leading domestic and international air carriers, and to establish Wayne County and the Detroit metro area as a regional transportation center.
HOK's design for the terminal combines the best in American operations technologies with an international blend of retail and service amenities. A central ticketing area serves as a gateway into the terminal. It features international-style ticketing banks, which organize ticket processing and check-ins by destination, grouped around centralized baggage belts to increase efficiency.
A central corridor leads passengers from the ticketing area to the terminal's Grand Hall, which contains retail shops, restaurants and other service amenities, including international duty-free shopping. Recalling landmark American and European train stations, the terminal's five-level Grand Hall is designed to serve as a hub of exchange and activity, as a passenger destination and meeting place. Its dramatic, light-filled open spaces highlight passenger activity while providing views of the airfields and of the sky above.
The design calls for five concourses leading to the individual passenger gates, four of which are served by people-movers reduce walking distances. A system of skylights provides natural lighting and directional orientation in the concourses.
HOK's design also includes a heavily landscaped access drive and a 6,000-car parking structure, which is connected to the terminal by bridges.

HOK は，ミシガン州デトロイトのウェイン郡空港に，ノースウェスト航空のための新しい旅客ターミナルを設計する指名コンペに招かれた．新しいターミナルは，ノースウェスト航空とブリティッシュ航空の国内線，国際線での主導的な航空会社としての立場の強化と地域の交通機関の中心を成すセンターとして，ウェイン郡とデトロイトの地下鉄網の確立を目的としている．

このターミナルは，アメリカの運営・管理技術と世界各国の小売店やサーヴィス施設をうまく結合させようとしたものである．中央のチケット・エリアはターミナルへのゲートとして機能する．国際様式のチケット・カウンターが並び，目的地別にチェック・インや発券を行う．カウンターは能率を上げるために荷物運搬用ベルト・コンベアを中央に設置しその回りに配置された．

中央通路がチケット・エリアからターミナルのグランド・ホールへ旅客を導く．そこはまた小売店やレストラン，その他のサーヴィス施設，世界各国の免税店も並んでいる．ランドマークとしてのアメリカやイギリスの列車の駅を想起させるターミナルの5層吹抜けのグランド・ホールは，両替や行動の中心として，また旅客到着や人との出会いの場として機能するよう設計されている．そのドラマティックで光に満ちたオープン・スペースは離着陸場や上に広がる空の眺めを楽しむことができる．

個々の旅客用ゲートへの五つのコンコースのうち四つは，ピープル・ムーヴァーを用いることで旅客の歩く距離を縮めている．スカイライトを採用した構成は，自然光を採り入れたり，コンコースの位置を知らせるのに役立っている．HOK の設計はまた多量の車の出入を可能にし，6,000台収容の駐車場を設け，ブリッジでターミナルとつないでいる．

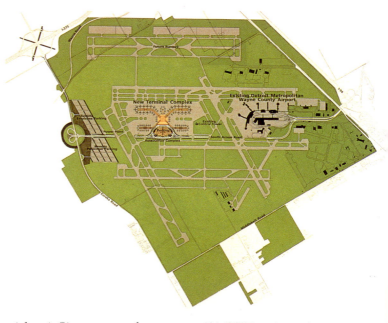

(above) Site master plan.
(p.215 from top to bottom)
Main level (departures) plan.
Mezzanine level (people-mover) plan.
Apron level plan.
Photo (p.216) by Kevin Lowder.

（上）配置図マスター・プラン．
(p.215上から下へ)
主階出発レヴェル平面図．
中2階（ピープル・ムーヴァー）平面図．
エプロン・レヴェル平面図．

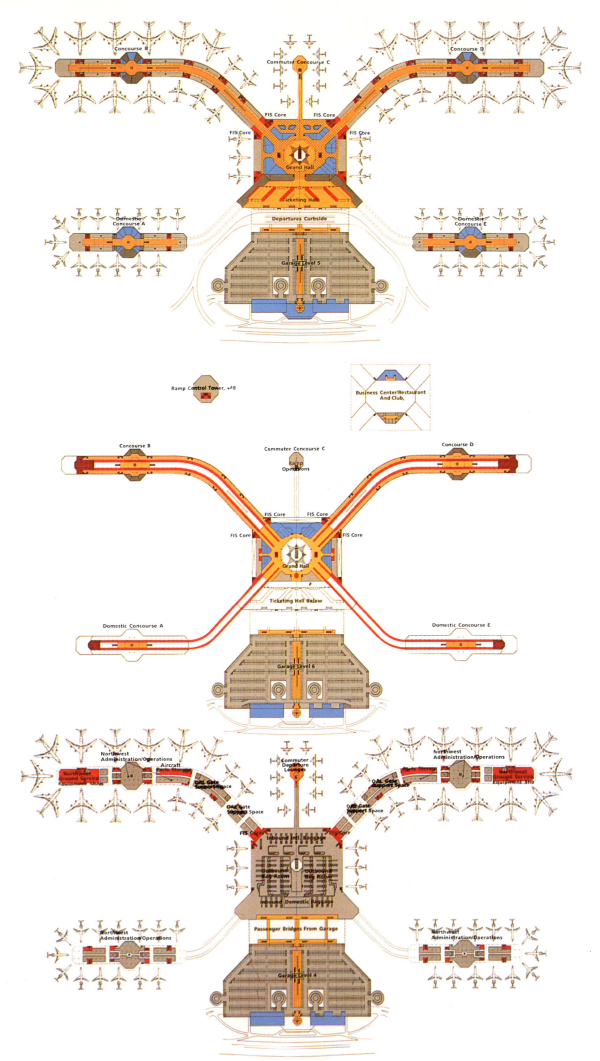

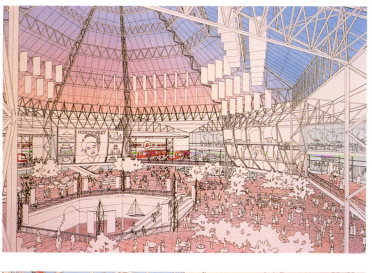

(p.216) Exterior view of
Northwest Airlines World
Travel Center.
(top) Grand Hall.
(above) Typical concourse,
showing people-mover tram
on the upper (mezzanine) level.

(p.216) ノースウェスト航空ワールド・
トラヴェル・センター外観.
（上）グランド・ホール.
（下）コンコース．上階にピープル・ム
ーヴァーが見える.

Foley Square
New York, New York, USA

フォーリィ・スクエア
アメリカ，ニューヨーク州ニューヨーク
(Recent Design Competition)

HOK recently submitted designs for two new federal buildings to the Foley Square Competition, sponsored by the General Services Administration. Foley Square has long served as the civic heart of New York City, providing the center for federal, state and municipal courts and administrative and judiciary services.

The buildings, One Foley Square and Two Foley Square, are designed to meet the growing needs of federal and municipal agencies and the federal court system. The expansion of this government complex will be the first major change in the area since the early 1970s.

HOK's design objective for both structures focuses on the creation of landmark buildings appropriate to federal and municipal uses, while complementing the surrounding historic structures.

One Foley Square

One Foley Square will be a 30-story Federal/Municipal Office Building containing public, retail and community facilities as well as federal and municipal office space. The 860,000-square-foot building is comprised of three basic elements: a setback tower, an enclosed public urban arcade and a special function pavilion east of the tower. The design of One Foley Square relates to adjacent buildings by establishing setbacks at corresponding heights and by creating an uninterrupted retail window base at ground level. The building has a solid granite base with limestone and granite accents above, enhancing its civic qualities.

共通役務庁主催によるフォーリィ・スクエア設計競技に，HOK は二つの連邦新庁舎の設計案を提出した．フォーリィ・スクエアは長い間ニューヨーク市の心臓部としての役割を果たしてきた．また，合衆国，州および市裁判所の中心であり，行政・司法の役割を担っている．
ワン・フォーリィ・スクエアおよびトゥー・フォーリィ・スクエアの建物は，連邦政府や市の部局，連邦裁判所の業務増加に応じるために計画される．この地域では政府の合同庁舎増築は，1970年代初期以来の計画である．この二つの建物に対する HOK の設計は，政府や市の施設にふさわしいランドマークとなる建築をつくり出すことにあり，周辺の歴史的建築物に沿うことである．

ワン・フォーリィ・スクエア

ワン・フォーリィ・スクエアは30階建ての連邦政府および市の事務庁舎となり，公共施設や店舗，コミュニティ施設も設けられる．延床面積は86万平方フィート，セットバックするタワー，アーケード，タワー東側のパヴィリオンからなる．ワン・フォーリィ・スクエアは隣接する建物にたいして，高さに応じてセットバックし，1階では店舗の開口部の位置をそろえて連続性をもたせる配慮がなされている．建物の基部は密実な花崗岩で，上部は石灰岩や花崗岩でアクセントがつけられ，この町の魅力を高めようとしている．

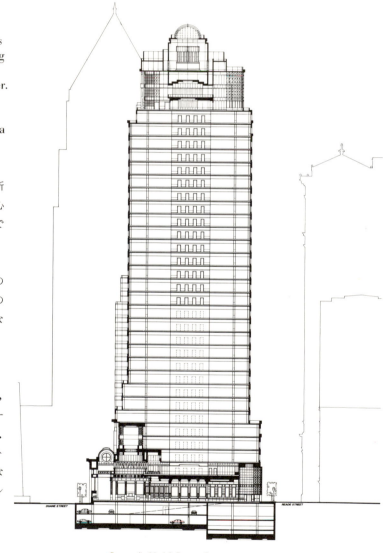

(above) Section.
(p.219) View from the east.
Photos (pp. 219, 220 and 223) by Roy J. Wright.

（上）断面図．
(p.219) 東からみた全景．

(top) U.S. Courthouse tower
is visible in the right end.
(above) Partial interior lobby
elevation.

（上）右端に連邦裁判所の塔が見える.
（下）ロビーの部分展開図.

Two Foley Square

The development of the new U.S. Courthouse, or Two Foley Square, will add 44 new federal courtrooms to alleviate overcrowded conditions at the existing U.S. Courthouse. The 29-story, 942,000-square-foot building is composed of two components: a tower which contains the courtrooms, judges' chambers and lounge, and a base which includes support spaces and offices for the Federal Courts.

Similar to adjacent courthouses, Two Foley Square will be clad in a predominantly warm gray granite with darker granite accents at the base. Where possible, window openings in the tower correspond to the functions within. For example, on east and west facades, 16-foot-high windows indicate the location of the courtrooms. At every third floor, the judges' chambers are clearly delineated with vertically-articulated windows. The overall composition concentrates the large stone surfaces to the center of the facades while increasing the glass at the corners. This treatment, when combined with the chamfered corners, carries the viewer's eye around the corner, thereby decreasing the perception of bulk and bringing it into harmony with the adjacent existing U.S. Courthouse tower.

トゥー・フォーリィ・スクエア

連邦裁判所あるいはトゥー・フォーリィ・スクエアの計画は44の新しい連邦法廷を増築して、現在の過密状態を多少とも解消しようとするものである。29階建て、94万2,000平方フィートのこの建物は、法廷、判事室、ラウンジのあるタワー、そして連邦法廷のための事務室や諸施設のある低層の基部からなる。

隣接する裁判所と同じように、トゥー・フォーリィ・スクエアも主として暖色のグレーの花崗岩が、アクセントとして基部には暗色の花崗岩が使われる。タワーの開口部は内部の機能によって表現されている。たとえば東西面では、高さ16フィートの窓は法廷の位置を示しているし、3階では判事室が縦長の窓で表されている。

全体の構成は、ファサードの中央部に花崗岩の壁面が集中し、隅部になるほどガラス面が多くなる。この方法は、面取りした隅部とつながると、人の視線を隅部に向かわせ、この建物の圧迫感を和らげ、隣に建つ既存の連邦裁判所の塔との調和を生みだす。

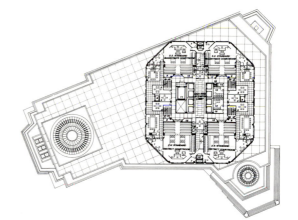

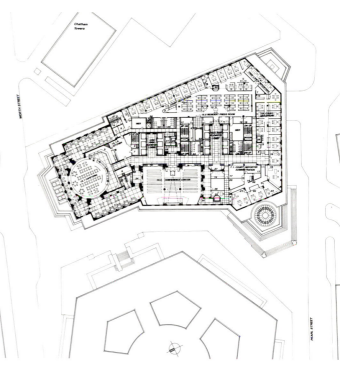

(from top to bottom)
District/magistrates Courts floor plan.
Eighth floor plan (cafeteria, conference center and press room, etc.)
Section.

（上から下に）
地方裁判所／微罪裁判所平面図。
8階平面図（カフェテリア、会議室、プレス・センターなど）。
断面図。

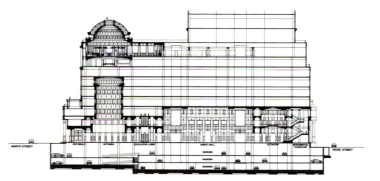

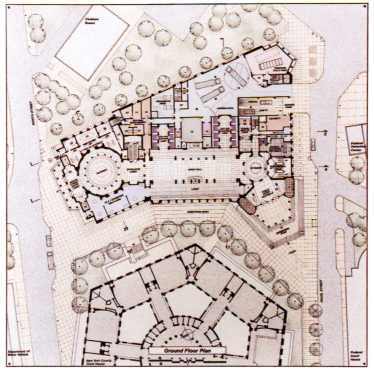

(p.222) West elevation.
(top) Harmony with the U.S.
Courthouse tower.
(above) Ground floor plan.

（p.222）西側立面図.
（上）連邦裁判所の塔との調和.
（下）1階平面図.

Biography of Gyo Obata

ギョー・オバタ略歴

Gyo Obata, the second of three children, was born in San Francisco in 1923, and raised in Berkeley, California.

His father, Chiura Obata, introduced the practice of Japanese ink painting, sumi-e, to the United States, and was a professor of art at the University of California at Berkeley. His mother, Haruko Obata, lives in Berkeley, where, at the age of 98, she continues to lecture and teach ikebana, the traditional Japanese art of flower arranging.

Obata's architectural training at the University of California at Berkeley was interrupted during his freshman year by the internment of Japanese-American citizens living in the western United States. In 1942, he was able to transfer to Washington University in St. Louis, where he graduated three years later with a bachelor of science degree in architecture.

Awarded a scholarship to study under Eliel Saarinen at the Cranbrook Academy of Art in Michigan, his graduate work culminated in a master plan for the city of St. Louis. He received a master's degree in architecture and urban design from Cranbrook in 1946.

He served briefly with the U.S. Army in the Aleutian Islands off the coast of Alaska before joining the Chicago firm of Skidmore, Owings & Merrill, where he worked for four years as a designer.

In 1951, he joined the St. Louis firm of Hellmuth, Yamasaki & Leinweber, and became principal in charge of design when that firm reorganized in 1955 as Hellmuth, Obata & Kassabaum. From a small firm with a staff of about two dozen, HOK today has become known throughout the world as one of the largest and most diverse design firms in the field of architecture, engineering and planning.

The sole remaining founding member, Obata currently serves as director of design as well as HOK's chairman, president, and chief executive officer.

Gyo Obata, a Fellow of the American Institute of Architects, has lectured on topics related to architecture and urban design, and has received numerous design awards. These include citations from the American Institute of Architects, the Urban Land Institute, the Federal Design Council, and the General Services Administration.

He makes his home in St. Louis, Missouri, where he and HOK were recently recognized for the significance of their contributions to the urban renewal of that city.

Photo by Will Crocket.

ギョー・オバタは，1923年，サンフランシスコに父チウラ，母ハルコの3人の子のうち2番目の子として生まれ，カリフォルニア州バークレーで育った．父チウラはアメリカに墨絵の仕事を伝えた．彼はカリフォルニア大学バークレー校の美術の教授だった．母ハルコは98歳の今，バークレーに住み，生け花を教えている．

ギョー・オバタは，バークレー校で建築を学びはじめた最初の年，アメリカ西部の日系アメリカ人収容に遭い，建築の勉強は中断された．1942年，彼はセントルイスのワシントン大学に移った．3年後，建築工学士として卒業した．奨学金を得て，ミシガン州のクランブルック美術アカデミーのエリエル・サーリネンのもとで学び，彼の卒業制作はセントルイスの都市計画マスター・プランになって実を結んだ．1946年，オバタはクランブルックで建築・都市計画の修士号を得た．

アラスカの沿岸から離れたアリューシャン列島で合衆国陸軍の兵役に服し，後にSOMシカゴ事務所に勤務，4年間デザイナーとして働いた．

1951年，ヘルムース・ヤマサキ・アンド・レインウェーバーのセントルイス事務所に勤務，1955年，この事務所がヘルムース・オバタ・アンド・カサバウムに組織替えになり，オバタは，デザインの責任者となった．24名の所員から出発し，HOKは今日，建築計画の分野で最大で多様な，世界でも有数の設計事務所として知られるようになった．

オバタは創設者としてただ一人今なお仕事をつづけ，HOKの会長，社長としてはもちろん，デザインの管理者としてその職責を果たしている．

彼はAIAの会員であり，建築や都市計画に関する話題について講演し，またこれまで多くの賞を受けている．これらには，AIA，アーバン・ランド協会，連邦デザイン評議会，共通役務庁からの授賞を含む．

ギョー・オバタはミズーリ州セントルイスを自分の故郷にしている．そこでオバタとHOKは，最近，セントルイスの都市再開発に重要な貢献をしたと認められた．

Chronological List of Gyo Obata/ HOK: 1954–

Date before 1990 (Academic Research Center) is year of building completion except Kansai International Airport. Date after 1990 (Plaza Indonesia) is year to be completed. "Future" is no date set for project completion.

1954

HOK is founded in St. Louis by George Hellmuth, George Kassabaum and Gyo Obata, with 24 employees.

Work
St. Sylvester Church
Eminence, Missouri, USA
N/A sf

(top and above)
St. Sylvester Church.

1956

In its first year, the firm more than doubles in size to 55 employees, and has $703,000 in net fees.

Work
Bristol Primary School
St. Louis, Missouri, USA
12,196 sf
photo by Ezra Stoller/Est

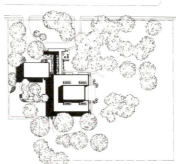

(top and above)
Bristol Primary School.

1957

Reflecting the postwar "Baby Boom," HOK's commissions include a number of new elementary and secondary schools.

Work
Warson Woods Elementary School
St. Louis, Missouri, USA
19,250 sf
photo by Ezra Stoller/Est

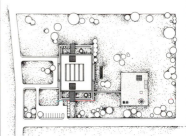

(top and above)
Warson Woods Elementary School.

1958

HOK completes a number of civic projects in Missouri, including a fire station headquarters built mostly underground in St. Louis.

Work
St. Louis Fire Alarm Headquarters Building
St. Louis, Missouri, USA
9,600 sf

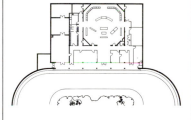

(top, middle and above)
St. Louis Fire Alarm Headquarters Building.

1962

As the children of the "Baby Boom" grow up, the firm's commissions include more secondary schools and university facilities. HOK now has 101 employees and more than $1 million in net fees.

Work
The Priory Chapel
St. Louis, Missouri, USA
130 acres 25,500 sf

(top and above)
The Priory Chapel.

1963

The Priory Chapel wins the top award in the annual "Design in Steel" competition.

Works
Mississippi University for Women Chapel
Columbus, Mississippi, USA
4,060 sf

Wohl Mental Health Institute
St. Louis, Missouri, USA
55,056 sf
photo by Mac Mizuki

(top)
Mississippi University for Women Chapel (The Carrier chapel).
(middle and bottom)
Wohl Mental Health Institute.

1964

HOK's annual net fees top $1.5 million. Projects completed this year include a development laboratory for IBM and the prison that replaced Alcatraz, the U.S. Penitentiary in Marion, Illinois.

Works
Berkeley Junior High School
Berkeley, Missouri, USA
55,945 sf
photo by Bill Engdahl of Hedrich-Blessing

IBM Advanced Systems Development Laboratory
Los Gatos, California, USA
80 acres 84,000 sf

Lindell Terrace Apartments
St. Louis, Missouri, USA
216,900 sf

United States Penitentiary Federal Bureau of Prisons
Marion, Illinois, USA
25 acres 334,100 sf

(from top to bottom)
Berkeley Junior High School.
IBM Advanced Systems Development Laboratory.
Lindell Terrace Apartments.

1965

Completed projects include two college facilities, a Nebraska monastery and new headquarters of the Missouri Conservation Commission.

Work
Missouri Conservation Commission Headquarters Office
Jefferson City, Missouri, USA
42 acres 30,000 sf

1966

HOK opens its second regional office in San Francisco and completes a major university project, the 2,600-acre campus of Southern Illinois University.

Works
Southern Illinois University Master Plan
Edwardsville, Illinois, USA
808,964 sf
photo by Barbara Martin

Washington University Dormitories
St. Louis, Missouri, USA
450,000 sf
photo by Bill Engdahl of Hedrich-Blessing

University of Wisconsin Parkside Campus Master Plan
Kenosha, Wisconsin, USA
690 acres 450,000 sf
photo by Kiku Obata

1967

HOK completes the new headquarters for the Federal Bureau of Reclamation in Denver.

Works
Avenue of the Stars Office Building
Los Angeles, California, USA
982,400 sf

Federal Bureau of Reclamation Engineering Center & Headquarters
Denver, Colorado, USA
60,000 sf
photo by Julius Shulman

LaBarge Inc. Office Building
St. Louis, Missouri, USA
30,000 sf
photo by Morley Baer

1968

With the addition of a regional office in Washington, D.C., the firm has 180 employees and net fees of nearly $3 million.

Works
CBS Gateway Tower Office Building
St. Louis, Missouri, USA
216,500 sf
photo by Morley Baer

United States Embassy
San Salvador, El Salvador
76,086 sf

(above)
Missouri Conservation.
Commisson Headquarters Office.

(from top to bottom)
Southern Illinois University Master Plan.
Washington University Dormitories.
University of Wisconsin Parkside Campus Master Plan.

(from top to bottom)
Avenue of the Stars Office Building.
Federal Bureau of Reclamation Engineering Center & Headquarters.
LaBarge Inc. Office Building.

(from top to bottom)
CBS Gateway Tower Office Building.
United States Embassy, San Salvador, El Salvador.

1969

HOK opens a regional office in Dallas, and completes a corporate headquarters for Ralston Purina Corporation in St. Louis. Gyo Obata is named a Fellow of the American Institute of Architects.

Works

Neiman-Marcus, The Galleria
Houston, Texas, USA
204,277 sf
photo by Ezra Stoller/Esto

Northwoods University of Michigan
Married Student Housing
Ann Arbor, Michigan, USA
89,000 sf

Ralston Purina
World Headquarters
St. Louis, Missouri, USA
295,000 sf
photo by Balthazar Korab

University of the West Indies
John F. Kennedy College of Arts and Sciences Master Plan
St. Augustine, Florida, USA
220,000 sf

1970

The firm has grown to 245 employees and more than $5 million in net fees.

Works

Pittsburgh Secondary School System
Pittsburgh, Pennsylvania, USA
265,000 sf

Psychoanalytic Foundation
St. Louis, Missouri, USA
37,000 sf

1971

HOK completes the Military Airlift Command Headquarters at Scott Air Force Base in Belleville, Illinois.

Works

Cornell University Dormitories
Ithaca, New York, USA
446,500 sf
photo by Alexandre Georges

Emerson Environmental Systems Building
St. Louis, Missouri, USA
167,023 sf

The Equitable Building Office and Commercial Development
St. Louis, Missouri, USA
507,180 sf
photo by Barbara Martin

1972

The U.S. General Services Administration (GSA) presents HOK with an Honor Award for the design of the National Air and Space Museum in Washington, D.C.

Works

University of Alaska Married Student Housing
Fairbanks, Alaska, USA
6.5 acres 50,000 sf
photo by Kiku Obata

Anthony's Restaurant, The Equitable Building
St. Louis, Missouri, USA
8,104 sf

University of Denver Penrose Library
Denver, Colorado, USA
125 acres 150,000 sf

Kimberly-Clark Research and Engineering Center
Menasha, Wisconsin, USA
102 acres 352,000 sf

Ozark National Scenic Riverways Site Analysis and Design Development
Carter and Shannon Counties, Missouri, USA
400 acres

E.R. Squibb & Sons, Inc. Corporate Headquarters and Research Facility
Lawrenceville, New Jersey, USA
273 acres 700,000 sf
photo by Norman McGrath

(top)
Neiman-Marcus. The Galleria.
(above) Ralston Purina.

(top and middle)
Pittsburgh Secondary School.
(above)
Psychoanalytic Foundation.

(from top to bottom)
Cornell University Dormitories.
Emerson Environmental Systems Building.
The Equitable Building.

(top) Married Student Housing.
(above) E.R. Squibb & Sons, Inc.

1973

The E.R. Squibb & Sons headquarters is named "Office of the Year" by *Administrative Management* magazine, "Laboratory of the Year" by *Industrial Research* magazine, and cited by *Architectural Record* in "Record Interiors of 1973."

Works

Bartlett Begich Junior/Senior High School
Anchorage, Alaska, USA
127 acres 323,924 sf

Missouri Botanical Garden John S. Lehmann Building Herbarium/Library
St. Louis, Missouri, USA
79 acres 50,000 sf
photo by Barbara Martin

(top) Bartlett Begich Junior/ Senior High School.
(above) Herbarium/Library.

1974

HOK now has 270 employees and more than $7.5 million in annual fees. The firm's design of the John S. Lehmann Building at the Missouri Botanical Garden receives the grand prize at the IBD/Interior Design competition.

Works

Community School Renovation
Ladue, Missouri, USA
18,600 sf
photo by Barbara Martin

Eagle River Correctional Center
Anchorage, Alaska, USA
207 acres 71,500 sf
photo by Kiku Obata

St. Louis Symphony Pavilion
St. Louis, Missouri, USA
40,000 sf

(from top to bottom)
Community School Renovation.
Eagle River Correctional Center.
St. Louis Symphony Pavilion.

1975

HOK has 368 employees and nearly $9.5 million in net fees.

Works

United States Marine Barracks
Washington, D.C., USA
228,190 sf
photo by Barbara Martin

Xerox Research Center
Palo Alto, California, USA
14 acres 110,000 sf
photo by Steven Dunham

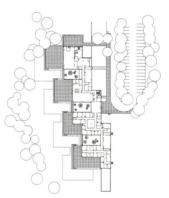

(top)
United States Marine Barracks.
(middle and bottom)
Xerox Research Center.

1976

Net fees top $15 million, and the firm opens a office in New York City. The National Air and Space Museum is completed and opens to large crowds.

Works

Boatmen's National Bank The Boatmen's Tower Office Building and Financial Complex
St. Louis, Missouri, USA
2 acres 626,918 sf

California State University Student Health Center
San Francisco, California, USA
30,000 sf
photo by Peter J. Henricks

General American Life Insurance National Service Center
St. Louis County, Missouri, USA
100 acres 68,300 sf

Incarnate Word Hospital Intensive Care Pavilion
St. Louis, Missouri, USA
73,300 sf

Laclede's Landing
St. Louis, Missouri, USA
24 acres

Village of Lake Placid Comprehensive Planning Services
Lake Placid, New York, USA
6 acres

Lubbock International Terminal Building
Lubbock, Texas, USA
2,500 acres 144,000 sf

National Air & Space Museum The Smithsonian Institution
Washington, D.C., USA
630,000 sf

One Northpark East Two Northpark East
Dallas, Texas, USA
40 acres 244,642 sf

(above)
Student Health Center.

1977

The Galleria, a pioneering mixed-use center, opens in Houston.

Works

Community Federal Center Corporate Headquarters
St. Louis, Missouri, USA
19 acres 364,000 sf
photo by Kiku Obata

The Galleria Mixed-Use Center
Houston, Texas, USA
33 acres 4,000,000 sf

King Saud University Master Plan
Riyadh, Saudi Arabia
2,400 acres 6,581,658 sf
Associate Architect:
Gollins Melvin Ward Partnership of London (Joint Venture)

Hulen Mall
Fort Worth, Texas, USA
50 acres 261,025 sf

Mallinckrodt Corporate Center
St. Louis, Missouri, USA
100 acres 122,000 sf

Vassar College Helen D. Lockwood Library
Poughkeepsie, New York, USA
32,000 sf
photo by Norman McGrath

(top)
Community Federal Center.
(above)
Library of Vassar College.

1978

George Hellmuth, one of the firm's founding partners, retires. He continues to serve as chairman of HOK's International Advisory Board.

Works

District of Columbia Courthouse
Washington, D.C., USA
700,000 sf

Dallas/Fort Worth International Airport
Arlington, Texas, USA
17,500 acres 1,207,000 sf
photo by George Silk

International Rivercenter Hilton Hotel
New Orleans, Louisiana, USA
23 acres 900,000 sf

Lenox, Inc. Corporate Headquarters
Lawrence Township, New Jersey, USA
12 acres 40,000 sf

The Olympic Center
Lake Placid, New York, USA
8,000 seats
6 acres 175,000 sf
photo by George Cserna

(from top to bottom)
D.C. Courthouse.
International Airport.
The Olympic Center.

1979

The firm has 574 employees and more than $20 million in net fees. HOK receives the Urban Land Institute's first annual award for the design of The Galleria.

Works

Belleville Area College
Belleville, Illinois, USA
213,300 sf

Marriot Corporation International Headquarters
Bethesda, Maryland, USA
33 acres 537,000 sf

University of Wisconsin Center for Health Sciences Master Plan
Madison, Wisconsin, USA
43 acres 800,000 sf
photo by Kiku Obata

Stanford University Cecil H. Green Library
Palo Alto, California, USA
180,000 sf
photo by Esto Photographics

Witte Hardware Building Renovation & Restoration
St. Louis, Missouri, USA
82,000 sf

(from top to bottom)
Center for Health Sciences.
Cecil H. Green Library.
Witte Hardware Building.

1980

HOK opens regional offices in Houston and San Diego, California, and brings in $25 million in net fees.

Works

Duke University Hospital and Research Institution
Durham, North Carolina, USA
770,000 sf
photo by Barbara Martin

Dulles International Airport Master Plan Update and Terminal Expansion
Chantilly, Virginia, USA
115,000 sf
photo by Allan Freeman

Mobil Oil U.S. Division Headquarters
Fairfax, Virginia, USA
130 acres 1,312,728 sf
photo by Hedrich-Blessing

Sheraton Washington Hotel
Washington, D.C., USA
16 acres 720,000 sf

Sun Bank Center Sun Bank Headquarters
Miami, Florida, USA
8 acres 300,000 sf

(from top to bottom)
Duke University Hospital and Research Institution.
Dulles International Airport.
Mobil Oil.

1981

Net fees top $35 million, and the firm now employs 797 people. The McDonnell Douglas Automation Center is named one of the "Ten Outstanding Engineering Achievements" by the National Society of Professional Engineers.

Works

GTE Advanced Management Education Center
Norwalk, Connecticut, USA
66 acres 205,000 sf

California Institute of Technology Thomas J. Watson Laboratories of Applied Physics
Pasadena, California, USA
40,000 sf
photo by Peter Aaron / Esto

George R. Moscone Convention Center
San Francisco, California, USA
11.5 acres 640,000 sf
Associate Architect:
Jack Young & Associates

Saks Fifth Avenue
San Francisco, California, USA
139,000 sf

Piers 1.2.3 Master Plan
Boston, Massachusetts, USA
19 acres 3,000,000 sf

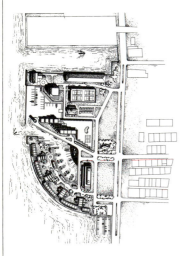

(top)California Institute of Technology.
(above)Piers 1.2.3 Master Plan.

1982

HOK closes its Belleville office and opens one in Denver. George Kassabaum, a founding partner, dies.

Works

University of Alabama Medical Center Master Plan
Birmingham, Alabama, USA
30 acres 1,500,000 sf

Echlin Manufacturing Company Headquarters Building
Branford, Connecticut, USA
17 acres 71,000 sf

Federal Reserve Bank of Richmond-Baltimore Branch
Baltimore, Maryland, USA
280,000 sf

University of Oklahoma Bizzell Memorial Library Doris W. Neustadt Wing
Norman, Oklahoma, USA
150,000 sf

Levi's Plaza
San Francisco, California, USA
11 acres 816,000 sf
photo by Peter Aaron/Esto

U.S. Embassy Staff Housing
Cairo, Egypt
197,196 sf

Missouri Botanical Garden Ridgway Center
St. Louis, Missouri, USA
79 acres 63,000 sf

Vanderbilt University Owen Graduate School of Management
Nashville, Tennessee, USA
101,000 sf

(top)Levi's Plaza.
(above)Vanderbilt University.

1983

HOK opens an office specializing in sports facilities in Kansas City, Missouri, and replaces its San Diego office with one in Los Angeles. Levi's Plaza is named one of the best designs of 1982 by *Time* magazine.

Works

Bay Area Rapid Transit System Regional Administrative Facility
Oakland, California, USA
106,559 sf

Exxon Research and Engineering Center
Clinton Township, New Jersey, USA
750 acres 900,000 sf

Sony Corporation of America Divisional Headquarters
Park Ridge, New Jersey, USA
38 acres 232,000 sf

Galleria Mixed-Use Center
Dallas, Texas, USA
44 acres 4,000,000 sf
Associate Architect:
Kendall/Heaton/Associates

King Khalid International Airport
Riyadh, Saudi Arabia
55,680 acres 3,332,124 sf

McDonnel Douglas Information Systems Group Computer Facilities
St. Louis, Missouri, USA
74 acres 1,062,000 sf
275,000 sf (computer)

One Oxford Centre
Pittsburgh, Pennsylvania, USA
4 acres 1,296,000 sf

(above)
Sony Corporation of America.

1984

HOK continues to expand, opening offices in Tampa, Florida, and Hong Kong. The firm has 873 employees and net fees of $44 million.

Works

Aetna Life & Casualty Group Division Headquarters
Middletown, Connecticut, USA
287 acres 1,200,000 sf

Damansara Town Center Mixed-Use Development Master Plan
Kuala Lumpur, Malaysia
54 acres 15,000,000 sf

First Interstate Bank of Utah Office Building and Bank Headquarters
Salt Lake City, Utah, USA
260,000 sf

King Khalid International Airport Interior Design
Riyadh, Saudi Arabia
6,581,658 sf

Phillips Point Mixed-Use Center
West Palm Beach, Florida, USA
3 acres 550,000 sf

The John L. McClellan Memorial Veterans' Hospital
Little Rock, Arkansas, USA
765,000 sf

Quorum Office Complex Master Plan
Addison, Texas, USA
72 acres 1,000,000 sf

Stanford University Cardiovascular Center
Palo Alto, California, USA
50,672 sf

Zale Corporation World Headquarters
Dallas, Texas, USA
50 acres 874,905 sf

(above)Quorum Office Complex.

1985

HOK receives the High Honors Award from *R&D* magazine for the Exxon Research and Engineering Center in Clinton, New Jersey. Net fees reach $53.4 million.

Works

Edison Brothers, Inc. Corporate Headquarters
St. Louis, Missouri, USA
630,000 sf

Fleet Center/Exchange Place Addition and Renovation
Providence, Rhode Island, USA
475,000 sf

Lake Merritt Plaza
Oakland, California, USA
1 acre 651,000 sf

Washington University School of Medicine Clinical Sciences Research Building
St. Louis, Missouri, USA
3 acres 382,080 sf

One Bell Center Southwestern Bell Corporate Headquarters
St. Louis, Missouri, USA
2 acres 1,460,907 sf

St. Louis Union Station Master Plan
St. Louis, Missouri, USA
35 acres 822,000 sf

Monsanto Life Sciences Research Center
St. Louis, Missouri, USA
21 acres 2,000,000 sf

The Emily Morgan Hotel Restoration and Renovation Interior Design
San Antonio, Texas, USA
130,000 sf
photo by Robert Miller

(above) The Emily Morgan Hotel.

1986

HOK receives the Grand Award for Engineering Excellence from the American Consulting Engineers Council for Riverchase Galleria.

Works

BP America, Inc. Corporate Headquarters
Cleveland, Ohio, USA
2.5 acres 1,508,000 sf

Kellogg Company Corporate Headquarters
Battle Creek, Michigan, USA
15 acres 500,000 sf

University of Minnesota Hospitals Renewal Project
Minneapolis, Minnesota, USA
557,947 sf

Riverchase Galleria
Birmingham, Alabama, USA
60 acres 1,192,000 sf

Merck & Co., Inc. Basic Research Laboratory
Rahway, New Jersey, USA
16 acres 263,000 sf

Trident Training Facility Naval Submarine Support Base
Kings Bay, Georgia, USA
338,000 sf
photo by Rion Rizzo

Saturn Corporation Manufacturing Facility Facility Programming
Spring Hill, Tennessee, USA
6,000,000 sf

(top) University of Minnesota Hospitals.
(above) Trident Training Facility.

1987

The Urban Land Institute presents its ninth annual Award for Excellence to HOK for the redevelopment of St. Louis Union Station.

Works

Fairmont Hotel
San Jose, California, USA
707,000 sf

Burger King Corporation World Headquarters
Miami, Florida, USA
114 acres 285,000 sf

B'nai Amoona Sanctuary Building Office and Education Facilities
St. Louis County, Missouri, USA
33 acres 27,500 sf
photo by George Cott

2405 Grand on Crown Square Office Tower
Kansas City, Missouri, USA
260,000 sf

The MCI Building Office Tower
St. Louis, Missouri, USA
278,000 sf

NCR Corporation Corporate Design Guidelines
Dayton, Ohio, USA

Plaza Building Phillips Petroleum Company Headquarters Complex
Bartlesville, Oklahoma, USA
2 acres 500,000 sf

Otis Elevator Research Tower and Marketing Facility
Bristol, Connecticut, USA
131,274 sf

Joe Robbie Stadium
Dade County, Florida, USA
73,000 seats 160 acres

The World Bank Office Building, "J" Building
Washington, D.C., USA
400,000 sf

Sacramento County Main Jail
Sacramento, California, USA
450,000 sf

(above) B'nai Amoona Sanctuary.

1988

The firm opens an office in London, and net fees top $100 million. HOK receives a Federal Design Achievement Award, the highest award given by the National Endowment for the Arts, for the redevelopment of St. Louis Union Station.

Works

Bradley Center Arena
Milwaukee, Wisconsin, USA
20,000 seats
4 acres 190,900 sf
Associate Architect:
Venture Architects

Case Western Reserve University Weatherhead School of Management
Cleveland, Ohio, USA
87,900 sf
photo by Robert Pettus

Fairmont Hotel
Chicago, Illinois, USA
793,812 sf
Associate Architect:
Fujikawa Johnson and Associates, Inc.

Forsythe Plaza at Union Station
St. Louis, Missouri, USA
600,000 sf

Kansai International Airport Design Competition
Osaka, Japan
Associate Architect:
Kajima Corporation
HOK Design Team:
Gyo Obata, William Valentine, Ernest Cirangle
Kajima Design Team:
Tuyoshi Okajima, Tomohisa Yuri, Hiroyuki Sakamoto

(top) Case Western Reserve University.
(above) Forsythe Plaza.

1988

Works

**Metropolitan Square
Luxury Office Tower**
St. Louis, Missouri, USA
1,531,817 sf

**National Air and Space
Museum
The Smithsonian Institution
Restaurant Addition**
Washington, D.C., USA
1 acre 38,000 sf

Hotel Nikko
Chicago, Illinois, USA
1 acre 422,000 sf

**Orange County Convention
and Civic Center**
Orlando, Florida, USA
525,000 sf
photo by George Cott

Pilot Field
Buffalo, New York, USA
40,000 seats

**New Orleans Centre at
the Dome
Mixed-Use Development**
New Orleans, Louisiana, USA
1,598,000 sf

**Prudential Center
Redevelopment Plan**
Boston, Massachusetts, USA
28 acres

Taipei World Trade Center
Taipei, Taiwan
16 acres 3,163,000 sf

**The Living World at
the St. Louis Zoo**
St. Louis, Missouri, USA
9.5 acres 55,000 sf

*(top) Orange County
Convention and Civic Center.*
(above)
Taipei World Trade Center.

1989

HOK completes two major
projects in its home town:
Metropolitan Square, the tallest
building on the St. Louis
skyline, and The Living World, a
high-tech education center at
the St. Louis Zoo. Gyo Obata
receives the Levee Stone Award
for his leadership in the renewal
of downtown St. Louis.

Works

**AT&T Irvine Center
Office Tower**
Irvine, California, USA
2,000 acres 325,000 sf
photo by Russell Abraham

**AmSouth/Harbert Plaza
Mixed-Use Center**
Birmingham, Alabama, USA
1.5 acres 701,925 sf
Associate Architect:
Gresham, Smith and Partners

**University of California at
Berkeley
Genetics and Plant Biology
Center**
Berkeley, California, USA
187,500 sf

(top)
*AT & T Irvine Center Office
Tower.*
(above)
*Genetics and Plant Biology
Center, University of California
at Berkeley*

1990

The firm, headed by founding
partner Gyo Obata, FAIA, has
nearly 1,000 employees in ten
offices located throughout the
United States and overseas.

Works

**801 Grand Avenue
Office Tower**
Des Moines, Iowa, USA
922,500 sf
Associate Architect:
Brook, Borg & Skiles

**Academic Research Building
J. Hillis Miller Health Center
University of Florida**
Gainesville, Florida, USA

**Plaza Indonesia and Grand
Hyatt Hotel and Retail
Complex**
Jakarta, Indonesia
11 acres 1,976,129 sf

1215K Office Tower
Sacramento, California, USA
245,000 sf

Londondome Events Center
London, England
25,000 seats
137 acres 204,000 sf

**Philadelphia Justice Center
Facility Programming Study**
Philadelphia, Pennsylvania, USA
700,000 sf

Tampa Convention Center
Tampa, Florida, USA
13.5 acres 580,000 sf

(top) Plaza Indonesia.
(above)
Londondome Events Center.

1991

Works

**Columbia University
Center for Engineering and
Physical Science Research**
New York, New York, USA
150,000 sf

**Wells Fargo Center at
the Capitol Mall**
Sacramento, California, USA
991,000 sf

Minami Office Tower
Las Vegas, Nevada, USA
600,000 sf

(top) Columbia University.
(middle) Wells Fargo Center.
(above) Minami Office Tower.

1992
Work
Camden Yards Twin-Stadium Complex
Baltimore, Maryland, USA

1993
Works
Cervantes Convention Center Expansion & Domed Stadium
St. Louis, Missouri, USA
432,449 sf
Associate Architect:
Kennedy Associates/Architects, Inc.
photo by Brian Kuhlmann

Reorganized Church of Jesus Christ of Latter Day Saints Temple
Independence, Missouri, USA
1,800 seats 130,000 sf

1997
Work
Kings County Hospital Center Expansion and Renovation
Brooklyn, New York, USA
40 acres 2,000,000 sf

Future
Works
Brickell Gateway Mixed-Use Complex
Miami, Florida, USA
7.5 acres 1,250,000 sf

New Comiskey Park Stadium
Chicago, Illinois, USA
45,000 seats 100 acres

Florida Museum of Natural History
Gainesville, Florida, USA
90,000 sf

Cranbrook Academy of Arts Facility Expansion Program and Master Plan
Bloomfield Hills, Michigan, USA
280 acres 1,088,000 sf

Tokushima Retirement Community Master Plan
Tokushima, Japan
320 acres 2,700,000 sf
Master Plan Completion: 1988

Imar Plaza
Design Competition
Istanbul, Turkey
4,500,000 sf

New York Hospital
New York, New York, USA
Associate Architect:
Taylor Clark Architects, Inc.

Foley Square
Design Competition
New York, New York, USA

Northwest Airlines World Travel Center
Design Competition in 1990
Wayne County Airport, Detroit, Michigan, USA
Associate Architects:
McClier Avitation Group, Greiner Engineering, and Nathan Johnson & Associates, Inc.

(top)
Cervantes Convention Center.
(above)
Reorganized Church of Jesus Christ of Latter Day Saints Temple.

(above)
Camden Yards Twin-Stadium Complex.

(top and above)
Kings County Hospital Center.

(top)
New Comiskey Park Stadium.
(above) Florida Museum.

Members of HOK

Office of the Chairman:

Gyo Obata
Chairman of the Board &
Chief Executive Officer

Jerome J. Sincoff
President &
Chief Operating Officer

King Graf
Vice Chairman

Robert E. Stauder
Vice Chairman

Board of Directors:

Gyo Obata
King Graf
Jerome Sincoff
Robert Stauder
Gerard Gilmore
Ronald Labinski
Patrick MacLeamy
Larry Sauer
Larry Self
Tad Tucker
William Valentine

Advisors to the Board:

Paul Watson, Secretary & Treasurer
John Mahon
Robert Pratzel

HOK Employees
as of September 1, 1990

Ernesto Abiva
Kathryn Ablan
Derwin Abston
Jenny Ackerman
Manuel Acoba
Kyoko Adachi
Scott Adams
James Adkins
Parthenopi Agathangelou
Trudi Agbowu
James Agne
Rose Mary Aiello
Kathleen Alberding
James Albertson
Eugenio Alday
Carrie Alexander
David Alexander
Sandra Allen
Robert Almanza
Ann Althoff
Joel Alves
David Amalong
Smari Amman
Tristan Anderson
Frank Anderson
Louise Angst
Don Apperson
Charles Armstrong
E. Taylor Armstrong
James Arthur
Celia Asprea
Pravin Assar
Robert Atchisson
Doris Atkinson
Robert Autry
Joselito Ayson
Carlos Ayuso
Julie Bachman
Susan Baerwald
M. Joseph Bahan
Pierre Baillargeon
James Ballenger
Ben Barnert
Paul Barnette
Donald Barnum, Jr.
Robert Barr
Barbara Barrier
Beth Barrier
Tracey Barrier
James Bartl
Mariano Bartolomei
Edward Bartz
Ed Bash
Muhammad Bashir
Nancy Basler
Leslie Bates
Frank Battipede
Colleen Baumgardner
Rolando Bautista
Bruce Beahm
Michael Beaudoin
Rhett Beavers
Deborah Beckett
Isobel Bedawi
Gregg Bedell
Carl Belden
Margie Bell
Amanda Benjamin
Arthur Benkelman
Michael Bennett
A. Lee Beougher
Linda Bernauer
Donald Berry
Richard Best
Diane Bickerton
Mark Binsted

Kimberly Bishop
Stephen Blackburn
William Blackwell, III
Robert Blaha
Tim Blair
C. William Blank, II
Larry Blankenship
Jeffrey Blydenburgh
Brad Blythe
Sharon Bobbitt
Peter Bobe
Faith Bolen
Tami Bolin
Sherri Boncek
Charles Booker, Sr.
Lisa Borowski
Ernest Borroel
Thomas Boshaw
David Botello
Cristina Bouri
David Bower
Mark Bowers
Jean Bowlin
Keith Bowman
Carolyn Boyd
J. Michael Brady
James Brakefield
Charles Brandau
Bharati Brandes
Robert Brandon
James Branham
Pamela Brannon
Wende Brasloff
Robert Braun
Steven Brewer
Alan Bright
Yuval Brisker
John (Tony) Brocato Jr.
Debra Brock
John Brockway
Donna Bromby
Janet Brown
Richard Brown
Duncan Broyd
Alton Broyles
Steven Brubaker
Lili Bruer
Elizabeth Brussel
Robert Bruyere
Russell Buchanan
J. Alan Buck
Barbara Budzinska
Madonna Buechel
Emmanuel Buenaventura
Jeraldean Bunn
Wilson Bunoan
Brad Burgoon
Mary Jo Burke
Michael Burke
William Burke
Thomas Burnham
Bryan Burns
Samir Burshan
Stevie Buthner
Harlan Cage
Jacqueline Calhoun
Wendy Callahan
Philip Callison
Gary Caltwedt
Cynthia Campbell
Hugh Campbell
Dionisio Canellas
Robert Canfield
Jerry Cannon
Kathy Cannon
Irlanda Cantu
George Canzoneri
Michael Capelle
Andrew Cappella

Mikeal Caraker
Cesar Cardona
Douglas Carr
Sandra Carrera
Jaime Carrion
Robert Carroll
Bobby Carter
Steven Carver
Joseph Casad
Celina Casillas
Frank Casso
Gwlynda Castro
Christopher Castrop
Brent Cato
Christopher Cedergreen
Blythe Cermak
Jen-Shen Chan
Kenneth Chan
Raymond Chandler
Yung Chang
Christine Chanteloup
Jeaneen Chapes
Michael Chapman
David Chassin
Nai Li (Larry) Chen
Raymond Cheng
Yeow Chia
James Chibnall
Sharon Chibnall
Jonathan Chiu
Helen Choi
Sze Chong
William Churchill
Ernest Cirangle
Anne Clark
Princeton Clark
Glenn Clarke
Wayne Clarke
Virgilio Co
Leesa Coller
Dana Collins
Cheryl Condon
Marilee Congrove
Linda Conley
John Conley
David Conner
Matthew Connolly
Clyde Conrad
Ed Coon, Jr.
Samuel Cooper
Dennis Cope
William Corneli
John Corson
David Cotner
Carol Covy
Jessica Crain
Dennis Cramer
Steven Crang
John Cravens
Charles Crawford, III
Craig Creason
Mark Critchfield
Barbara Cronn
J.R. Crowell
Rodney Crumrine
Primitivo Dadivas
Patricia Daley
Philip Dangerfield
Michael Dant
Erin Dare
Theodore Davalos
Clark Davis
Cynthia Davis
Jerry Davis
Mary DeBold
Vicki Deemie
Richard deFlon
Roberto De Guzman
Craig Deister

Kimberlee DeJong
Michael Del Sordo
Michael Delano
Patrick Delano
Ed DeLara
Timothy Delorm
Pamela DelVecchio
Dwight Demay
Douglas Demers
Debbie Dempsey
Joseph Desalvo
Guy Despatis
Bertha Dickerson
Andrew Dickie
George Dickie
Judith Diehl
Rosanna Dill
David Dimitry
Nan Doelling
Daniel Dolan
Janice Dooley
Thomas Doremus
Charles Dorn
Richard Dowd
Lisa Dozier
Judy Du Buque
Robert Ducker
Gregory Duda
Stephen Duda
Michael Duddy
Paul Duell
Andrew Duffy
Paul Dunn
Mary Dunsford
Katharine Dunton
Kyle Dupre
Philip Durham
Jerry Duval
Randy Dvorak
Brendan Dwyer
Robert Edmunds
Judy Edwards
Frank Effland
Jane Eickelberg
Sherry Eisenberg
Donald Elliott
Michelle Ellis
Graham Elswick
Carolyn Emmons
Bon Eng
David Eng
Therese' Engel
Stephen England
Tyler Engle
Susan English
Gerald Equi
Frank Erbschloe, Sr.
Frank Erbschloe, Jr.
Glennon Erney
Stewart Ervie
Michael Ervin
Julia Esparrago
Marco Esposito
Joseph Esser
Glen Essink
Esther Estrada
Iliana Estrada
Francis Etro, Jr.
Connie Etzel
Doug Etzel
Phillip Evans
Stephen Evans
Anthony Eves
James Fair
Mark Farmer
Brian Farnsworth
Rich Farris
Kevin Fast
Robert Fatovic

Michael Fejes
Alemtsehay Ferede
Marilyn Feris
Ramon Fernandez
James Fetterman
Rick Fiebig
Robert Fingland
Allan Fleischman
Alicia Flores
Rosie Flores
Kimberly Folse
Ronald Ford
Deborah Formato
Robert Forney
Susan Forquer
Nondus Fortner
Angela Fowler
Linda Fowler
Diane Fox
Donald Francke
Charles Frank
Claudine Frasch
Kelly Fray
Curtis Frey
Kimberly Frey
Corinna Fritsch
Christopher Fromboluti
Ronald Frost
Jeffrey Fucigna
Denise Fuehne
Kecia Fuller
Loretta Fulvio
Gayle Furuta
Jamie Gagliarducci
Shawn Galbreath
Cresencio Garcia
Russell Garcia
Diane Gartner
Glenn Gee
Charles George
Christine George
Michael Gilbreath
David Gile
John Gilliam, III.
Gerard Gilmore
Gordon Gilmore
John Gilmore
Michael Giltenane
Wayne Glover
David Gnaegy
Allan Gober
Louis Gogue
Micki Goldberg
Missy Goldberg
Nancy Goldburg
Gary Golden
Jane Gomery
Pat Gonzales
Noel Gonzalo
Lee Good
Trudy Goode
Tawn Gorbutt
Rachel Gordon
Makio Goto
Kimberly Gottfredson
Thomas Goulden
King Graf
Bevin Grant
Charlene Gravel
Donald Gray
Andres Grechi
John Greenlee
Keith Greminger
Michael Griebel
Paul Griesemer
John Griffin
Deborah Griffin
Dimitri Guerriero
Raymond Guhe

Gaudencio Guintu, Jr.
Jonathan Guze
Stan Haas
Brenda Hacklander
Steven Hackman
Mark Haddock
Duane Hafley
Farzine Hakimi
Frank Hall
Kim Hall
David Halpern
Clifford Ham
David Hamill
Gary Hamman
Christine Hammer
Joseph Hampson
Joseph Hannah, Jr.
Richard Hannigan
Kenneth Hanser
Richard Hanusek
Vicki Hardesty
Lynnette Hardy
Jan Harmon
James Harrington
Rhonda Harris
Sara Harrison
Phoebe Hart
Steven Hartke
Craig Hartmann
Tom Hasemeier
Basil Hassan
Rhonda Hayes
Laura Heator
Hans Hecker
Marilyn Hecker
Kathleen Heimerman
Matt Heinicke
George Heinlein
George Hellmuth
Scott Hemlock
Charles Henderson
Aliece Hendricks
Shirley Henn
James Henrekin
Marvin Henrie
Ronald Herbig
Patricia Hercules
Kenneth Herold
C. Michael Herring
Randie Hersh-Fager
Ramona Hess
Donald Hesse
Roger Hibbeler
Kenton Higgins
Constance Hildesley
Frederick Hill
Robert Hill
Julie Hillemeyer
Jack Hipps, Jr.
Kurt Hobson
Lyle Hodgin
Jonathan Hoffschneider
Terri Hogan
Julie Holbert
Jill Holland
Kenneth Hollifield
Jerry Holmes
Thomas Holthaus
Pamela Holzapfel
Bill Homrighausen
Charles Hook
George Hoover
Tracy Hopkin
Christopher Hornbeck
Bruce House
Charles Howard
Kenneth Howell, Jr.
Lawrence Hrbek, Jr.
Dee Hrebosky

Sandi Hubbard
Nathan Huebner
Scott Hueting
Yee Huey
Robb Hult
Suzanne Hunter
Samuel Hyatt
Gary Illidge
Phyllis Infanzon
Charles Ingrum
Pauline Irwin
Nathan Isley
Zuraimi Ismail
Molly Jacks
Steve Jackson
Reuben Jacobs
Daniel Jacoby
Bob Jalilvand
Susan James
James Jamis
Krunica Janovic
Fred Jaross
Randal Jasper
Daniel Jeakins
Kendra Jeffries
Robert Jensen
William Jeorling
Sue Jochens
Lawrence Joe
Leslie Johns
Sharon Johnson
Edwin Johnson
Eric Johnston
David Joiner
Jerald Joiner
Paul Jolly
Dale Jones
Danny Jones
Ruth Jones
H. Creighton Jones
Krunica Jonovic
Andrew Jose
Thomas Kaczkowski
Harold Kallaway
Christian Kapl
Pete Karamitsanis
Robert Karamitsos
Steven Karr
Curtis Katterhenry
Cynthia Keeffe-Moelder
Larry Keen
James Kellogg
John Kelly
Janet Kelley-Harmon
Dan Kennaley
Stephen Kennedy
Phyllis Kenward
James Kessler
Ronald Kessler
Gerald Kettler
Khairina Khairuddin
Nada Kiblawi
John Killar
Hamilton Kilpatrick
John King
Terry Kingston
Ian Kinman
Rita Kistler
Kathy Kleinhans
G. Gene Klevanov
Susan Klumpp
Jonathan Knight
Susan Knoll
Gary Knoll
Scott Knoll
Nancy Kodukula
James Koentopp
Allison Kohler
Debora Kolb

Herbert Koopman
Richard Korvick
John Kouletsis
Rita Kozek
John Kraskiewicz
Joseph Kresslein
Robert Krohn
Christine Kwak
Ismail Kutluer Kwendeche
Antonio La Rosa
Al Labbee
Michelle Labinski
Ronald Labinski
William Lacey
Dennis Laflen
Terry Laflen
Daniel Lam
Anthony Lamitola
Margaret Landry
Sandra Landry
James Larkins
Mary Lazarus
Cheryl Leahy
P. James LeBlanc
Angela Lee
Monique Lee
Michael Lehman
Rodney Leibold
Joel Leider
Leslie Lenart
Ronald Lentz
Edmund Leo
Douglas Leonard
John Lesire
Grace Leung
Sally Leung
Steven Leuthold
Janet Lewinski
Samuel Lewis
Doris Lewis
Shoou-Chang Liang
Frank Liebgott
Steve Liescheidt
Chwee Lim
Yvonne Lim
Shyr-Yann Lin
Michael Lischer
Sara Liss-Katz
Angelo Logan
Debra Logan
Ann Lok
Susan London
William Long, Jr.
Theodore Lopez
Donald Loudermilk
F. Bryan Loving
Edwin Low
John Lowe
Deborah Lowes
William Luecking
Karen Luttrell
Werner Maassen
Stuart MacDonald
Richard Macias
Catharina MacKay
Patrick MacLeamy
Etsuko Maeda
Viola Magee
John Mahon
Tara Mahoney
Helen Maib
Laura Mainini
Susanne Majesky
Larry Malcic
James Malench
Brenda Mallonee
Mary Maloney
Mark Maloy
Dorene Maniccia

Patrice Marchal
Marti Mark
Susan Marney
Terence Marolt
Cristina Marotto
Bruce Marshall
John Martha
Nancy Martin
Philip Martin
Richard Martin
James Martin
Scott Martin
Luis Martinez
Leonard Marvin
Jean Masterson
Toretta Matthews
Terry Mattison
Linda Mayberry
Ann Mayer
Paul Mayer
Donald McAtee
Laura McCanna
Cindy McCarthy
Joseph McCauley
James McClellan
John McClelland
Mary McCormack
Shirley McCormack
Lisa McCracken
Cynthia McCune
Thomas McCune
Adela McDonald
Anna McGarrell
Edward McGrail
John McGuire
Mary McIntyre-Hair
Magda McKearin
Kent McLaughlin
Robert McLemore
Kathleen McManamon
Carole McMullen
Richard McPherson
Monica Melvin
Kobla Mensa-Kuma
Lisa Mercurio
J. Foard Meriwether
Deborah Messina
Terence Meurk
Craig Meyer
Gary Miciunas
Bruce Miller
Kyleen Miller
Lyle Miller
Kirk Millican
Michael Mindlin
Darrell Miner
Elizabeth Minor
Romero Miraflor
Rosemary Miramontes
Clark Mleynek
Ali Moghaddasi
Kenneth Mohr, Jr.
James Moler
Robert Moon
Lesley Morgado
Larry Moseley
Hing Moy
Eric Moy
Veronica Moynihan
Rawia Mudaris
Gerald Mueller
Rolf Muenter
Carl Mukri
Teresa Mulford
Daniel Mullin
David Munson
Carole Murphree
Sean Murphy
Marilyn Mussman

William Mykins
Robert Nachtrieb
Paul Nagashima
Arthur Nakamura
Vicky Nappier
Marcia Navarre
Julia Nazar
Dale Nederhoff
Peter Needle
G. Dennie Neilson
Suzanne Neistat
James Nelson
Thomas Nelson
Ann Newsham
James Ng
Minh Nguyen
Deborah Nicholson
Susan Niculescu
Kathryn Nigl
Craig Noreen
Larry Norris
Cynthia O'Brien
Mark O'Brien
Gerard O'Donovan
Peter Ohlhausen
John O'Mara
Robert O'Shaughnessy
Gen Obata
Gyo Obata
William Odell
Nick Ogura
Mark Oldham
Julian Ominski, Jr.
Charles Oraftik
Reynaldo Ortega
Donald Osbourn
Robert Osgood
Jacek Ostoya
Mark Otsea
Debra Outlaw
Don Overmyer
Enrick Padua
Jon Paget
Rosalind Paguio
Mark Palmer
William Palmer
Virginia Panky
Richard Panos
James Paplomatas
Je-Yu Park
Steve Parker
Amadeo Pasia
Patricia Payne
Jon Pearson
Richard Peat
Robin Pendleton
Daniel Perez
Donald Peters
Jaroslaw Petruscak
Lois Pezzi-Rapoport
David Pfund
Cheryl Phillips
Daniel Phillips
Mark Piaia
James Pieper
Shawn Pierce
Dorothy Pierson
Nancy Pijut
Thomas Pinkerton
Lalida Pinsuvama
Steven Pitt
Amanda Pitt
Teresa Pitt
Scott Pittman
Michael Plumtree
Roy Poggianti
Joyce Polhamus
Derrel Poole
Michael Popp

Jesus Porras
Lynn Potts
Richard Powers
Robert Powers
Bernadine Prater
Robert Pratzel
Christopher Preovolos
Brigitte Preston
Michael Preston
Erik Prochnik
Susan Pruchnicki
Anne Pundyk
Janis Purgalis
Marcel Quimby
Yonko Radonov
Arthur Ramirez
Jay Ramirez
Gerard Ramos
Patricia Ramsey
Joan Rangus
Jagdish Raote
Joe Rapisardo
Alexis Rappaport
Ripley Rasmus
Paul Ratnofsky
Margaret Re
Elizabeth Reatiraza
Charles Reay
William Reehl
Robin Reich
Stepan Rektorik
Rita Renshaw
David Retzsch
Steven Reynolds
Fershelia Richardson
Quintin Richardson
James Richert
Virginia Rimmer
Gregory Ripley
Russell Robertson
Mary Roche
Manuel Rodriguez
Rene Rodriguez
Edward Roether
Thomas Rogers
Kathleen Rogers
Hermann Roschen
David Ross
Danny Rothe
Lisa Rovner
Elva Rubio
Larry Rugg
Dennis Runyan
Curt Ruppel
Paul Rybalka
Philip Salembier
Theresa Sandoval
Earl Santee
Migdalia Santiago
Lisa Santschi
Dominic Sarica
Ganesh Sathyan
Larry Sauer
Lynn Saunders
Joyce Saunders
Mark Schantz
Michele Schellhardt
Rose Schillinger
Lynne Schirmer
Leah Schleifer
Diana Schlessinger
Karen Scholiltz
Melody Schreppel
Michael Schuetz
John Schulte
Vicky Schumacher
Kem Schwartz
Rebecca Schwartz
Robert Schwartz

Joseph Scolaro
Pamela Scott
Gina Scotti
Paul Scovill
Anthony Scullen
Patrick Seamans
John Secleter
Kirit Sedani
Paul Sedovic
Thomas See
Larry Self
Brian Seufert
Lorri Shafer
Eleanor Shams
Zaigham Shariff
Lowell Shepherd
Kelly Sheridan
Mary Sheridan
George Shotts, Jr.
Charles Siconolfi
Alisa Siegel
Caroline Silch
Julia Simet
Donal Simpson
Jerome Sincoff
Surrinder Singh
Margaret Sinnett
Pat Slaven
Steven Slosek
James Sloss
Robin Smead
Dawn Smith
Dayle Smith
Gregory Smith
Haden Smith
Marsha Smith
Douglas Smith
Jamie Smith
Lewell Smith
Stewart Smith
Charles Smith III.
Louis Soliz
John Soraci
Maura Sordo
Roger Soto
Ramona Soto
Raymond Soya
Jimi Soyebo
Tobi Spacil
Ted Spaid
Leneva Sparks
J. Stanley Sparks
Sam Spata
Jeffrey Spear
Joseph Spear
Mark Sperberg
Laurie Sperling
Bruce Sprenger
Kyle St. Peter
Robert Stauder
Julie Steele
James Stehr
Archie Stephens
Michael Stern
Robert Steul
Susan Stika
William Stinger
Robert Stockdale
Jean Stogner
Joan Stout
Peter Strauss
Tina Straw
John Strickland
Wayne Striker
Charles Stringer
Jeff Strohmeyer
Mary Stubler
Janice Suddath
Peder Sulerud

Kenneth Sussman
David Suttle
Christine Svetlecic
Steven Swanson
Roberta Swatek
Jennifer Sweeney
Richard Sweeney
Max Swider
M. James Swords
Conswaila Sydnor
Samuel Sylvester
James Takagi
Kevin Takeda
Sahoko Tamagawa
Patrick Tangen
Susan Tansill
Jennifer Tate
Jeanne Tauser
Owen Taylor
Robert Taylor
Michael Tchoukaleff
Paul Tchoukaleff
Richard Tell
Kendrick Tella
Alan Temple
Stephen Templeton
Sylvia Teng
Eve Tennenbaum
Jenelle Terry
Steven Terusaki
Janice Thorup
Brenda Tolley
Marc Tomlinson
Robert Towell
Alec Trickey
Patsy Trine
Lisa Troehler
Bryan Trubey
Marek Tryzybowicz
Lila Tsuda
Alan Tucker
Tad Tucker
John Turmelle
Donald Kent Turner
Karenina Turner
Timothy Tynan
James Tyner
Erik Ulland
Laura Underwood
Jill Unger
Walter Urbanek
Thomas Usher
William Valentine
Rajesh Valluri
Rose Marie Valte'
James Van Hook
Julie Vangelakos
Darren Varner
Debby Vaughan
Monique Veraart
Anne Voline
James Waggoner
Steve Wagley
Carlton Wagner
Henry Walkenhorst
Andre Walker
Kathleen Walker
Patty Walker
Sharon Walker
Susan Walker
Andrew Walleck
James Walters
Carolyn Ward
Robert Watel, Jr.
Jackson Waterbury
Bradley Waters
Paul Watson
Gilbert Watts
Dana Waymire

Daniel Weber
Kathleen Weber
Gary Wehmeier
Douglas Wehrle
Myron Weimer
Colin Weiner
Carla Weinheimer
Stephanie Weiss
Lisa Welgehausen
Dennis Wellner
Martin Wendel
Till Wendel
Michael Westerheid
Martha Whitaker
Marion White
Richard White
David Whiteman
Sue Wiest
William Wilcox
David Williams
Debbi Williams
Donald Williams
Jesse Williams
Louis Williams
Hugh Williamson
Julie Willman
Jeannette Wilmot
Harvey Wilmoth
Pamela Wilson
Henry Winkelman, Jr.
Norton Wisdom Jr.
Jamie Wise
Eric Wobbe
Judith Wohltman
Alan Wolf
Peter Wolfe
James Wolterman
Andrew Wong
Pichai Wongwaisayaw
David Wood
Edgar Wood
Richard Wood
Chandler Woods
Donald Wootton
Steven Worthington
Beverly Wrobel
John Wunsch
Evan Wykes
Richard Yaw
Anna Young
Daniel Young
Patricia Yovanovich
Zhiling Yu
Olga Zhovreboff
Robert Zielinski
William Ziervogel
Floyd Zimmerman
Allan Zreet
Augustine Zuniga
Christine Zvokel

● au 既刊臨時増刊号

ルイス・カーン──その全貌　1975年10月　品切れ

ポール・ルドルフ作品集──1946-74年/作品100題　1977年7月　品切れ

アントニオ・ガウディ──石の中に構築された建築的ヴィジョン　1977年12月

チャールズ・W・ムーア作品集　1978年5月　品切れ

ポスト・モダニズムの建築言語　チャールズ・ジェンクス　1978年10月

フィリップ・ジョンソン作品集　1979年6月　品切れ

ロブ・クリエの都市と建築のタイポロジー　1980年6月

転換するアメリカ現代建築　1981年3月　品切れ

フランク・ロイド・ライトと現代　1981年7月　品切れ

ロバート・ヴェンチューリ作品集　1981年12月　品切れ

ロバート・A・M・スターンの住宅・インテリア　1982年7月

アルド・ロッシ作品集　1982年11月

アルヴァ・アアルト作品集　1983年5月

ルイス・カーン──発想と意味　1983年11月

エーロ・サーリネン作品集　1984年4月

ハンス・ホライン作品集　1985年2月

シーザー・ペリ作品集　1985年7月

カルロ・スカルパ作品集　1985年10月

チャールズ・ジェンクス──象徴的建築をめざして　1986年1月

ヘルムート・ヤーン作品集　1986年6月

マリオ・ボッタ作品集　1986年9月

サイト：ナラティヴ・アーキテクチュア　1986年12月

ニューヨーク・アール・デコ・スカイスクレイパーズ　1987年4月

IBA：ベルリン国際建築展　1987年5月

ケヴィン・ローチ作品集　1987年8月

建築：光の詩学　ヘンリィ・プラマー　1987年12月

イタリア建築　1945-1985

フランチェスコ・ダル・コォ／セルジョ・ポラーノ編　1988年3月

アメリカ高層建築　1988年4月

ノーマン・フォスター作品集：1964-1987年　1988年5月

ピーター・アイゼンマン作品集　1988年8月

リチャード・ロジャース作品集：1978-1988年　1988年12月

レンゾ・ピアノ作品集：1964-1988年　1989年3月

アルヴァロ・シザ作品集：1954-1988　1989年6月

可能性の住宅　1989年9月

ピーター・クック：1961-1989　1989年12月

スターリング／ウィルフォード作品集　1990年5月

20世紀の建築と都市：パリ

J.L.コーエン／M.エルブ／A.マルティネリ　1990年9月